100 WARRINGTON
GREATS   RUGBY LEAGUE FOOTBALL CLUB

Four stars: Four Warrington greats are pictured climbing down the thirty-nine steps at Wembley after receiving the Challenge Cup in 1950. Leading from the front is captain Harry Bath, followed by scrum-half Gerry Helme and full-back Les 'Cowboy' Jones with winger Albert Johnson at the back.

100 GREATS

WARRINGTON
RUGBY LEAGUE FOOTBALL CLUB

WRITTEN BY
EDDIE FULLER AND GARY SLATER

TEMPUS

First published 2002
Copyright © Eddie Fuller and Gary Slater, 2002

Tempus Publishing Limited
The Mill, Brimscombe Port,
Stroud, Gloucestershire, GL5 2QG

ISBN 0 7524 2414 9

Typesetting and origination by
Tempus Publishing Limited
Printed in Great Britain by
Midway Colour Print, Wiltshire

Field of dreams: Warrington vice-president Clarrie Owen with Wilderspool Stadium forming a familiar backdrop.

Introduction

As vice-president of Warrington Wolves Rugby League Football Club, I was delighted when Eddie Fuller and Gary Slater asked me to write the introduction to this, their second book. Like the first, *Warrington Rugby League Club 1970-2000*, published two years ago, I am sure it will bring memories flooding back for generations of supporters.

I saw my first match at Wilderspool in the winter of 1932 and even now, almost seventy years later, the club and the sport remain an important part of my life. I can't remember who the Wire were playing that afternoon, but I soon got to know the names of the players – men like the Cumbrian full-back Billy Holding and the rugged centre Bill Shankland. Shankland was my first hero because he was the captain of the team and he had come all the way from Australia in 1931, just to play for us.

Me and my pals used to stand in the boys' pen behind the posts at the Spion Kop End of the ground. It cost us 3d to get in. In those days, the players still got changed in a wooden hut at the Fletcher Street End. It was another couple of years before the changing rooms in the main stand were opened and the players' tunnel was hollowed out of the ground. Almost immediately, of course, it flooded and that remained a problem for years to come.

At the end of my first season as a supporter, Warrington reached the Challenge Cup final against Huddersfield at Wembley. I could not afford to make the trip to London and so listened to the match on the radio, clutching a copy of the *Radio Times*, which contained a plan of the pitch divided into eight squares. Alongside the commentary, another voice would say 'square two' and so you could tell how close Huddersfield were to the Warrington try-line.

Billy Dingsdale was one of the Warrington try-scorers that day, and I believe that he and Bryn Knowelden, whom we signed from Barrow after the war, were the two brainiest, football-minded centres the club have ever had.

People often ask me what my most memorable match is and I always cite the Challenge Cup final replay against Halifax at Odsal Stadium in May 1954, if only because an occasion like that could never happen again. The official attendance was 102,575 but another 20,000 fans were stuck in traffic, listening to the match on the radio.

I was running fourteen coaches to the game from outside the Lord Rodney pub, but by the time we got in the ground, the score was already 3-0. We had missed Jim Challinor's opening try. However, I well remember Gerry Helme's clinching score in the second half when he collected the ball from a scrum forty yards out and dummied to pass to winger Stan McCormick twice before touching down in the corner.

But every game has been memorable for one reason or another. I vividly recall a Challenge Cup tie at Salford in February 1937 when Salford were one of the best teams in the country and we were given no chance of winning. I was about fourteen years old and it was one of my first away games.

It was bitterly cold, the pitch was muddy and the ball was heavy. When the Salford scrum-half fed the ball at a scrum, he deliberately threw it into the face of Dave Cotton, the Warrington hooker. Suddenly, Cotton's fist emerged from the scrum and flattened him. He was out cold for a couple of minutes. Cotton and second-row forward Jack Arkwright, the Warrington captain at the time, were hard men, playing a tough game in difficult conditions.

After the war I was fortunate enough to see Brian Bevan make his debut for Warrington's A team against Widnes A at Wilderspool in November 1947. Bevan had a quiet first forty minutes but, in the second half, he raced after a kick to score a perfectly good try in the corner. The referee, however, disallowed it because he did not believe that anybody could run that fast. Bevan, of course, could and did, and, in my opinion, he is the best back Warrington have ever had. The best forward would have to be Les Boyd. He was a perfect gentleman off the pitch, but an absolute animal on it.

I also saw Alex Murphy make his debut for St Helens. The story at the time was that Vince Karalius, the Saints loose-forward, had told young Alex to touch down for his tries at the side of the posts, not between them, to prevent his head from getting stuck. Murphy, however, was a lovable rogue and an outstanding player, who always seemed to outwit and out-think the referee.

Warrington's best goalkicker would have to be Steve Hesford, but who could forget the seven goals that Derek Whitehead kicked at Wembley to win us the Challenge Cup in May 1974?

From 1983 until 1991, I was on the Warrington board and was the director of scouting responsible for signing thirty-five young players, twelve of whom went on to play for the Great Britain under-21 side. Company law meant that I had to stand down when I reached the age of seventy. However, I remained a close friend of the board and when Sam Shepherd, the former grade one referee from Oldham, told me about two promising schoolboys, I passed their names on to Peter Higham, the then Warrington chairman.

They were Iestyn Harris and Paul Sculthorpe. Both signed for Warrington, went on to play for Great Britain and have received the coveted Man of Steel award, given annually to the personality who has had the most impact on the season.

All the Warrington players I have mentioned above and many more, like Bob Ryan, Parry Gordon, John Bevan and Ken Kelly, are featured in this volume. I am sure you will enjoy reading about their exploits in the famous primrose and blue jersey.

Clarrie Owen
Vice-president Warrington Wolves Rugby League Football Club.

Acknowledgements

Special thanks must go to the Warrington Museum and Art Gallery for granting access to the remarkable scrapbooks compiled by Jackie Hamblett during his sixty years as Warrington groundsman; to the *Warrington Guardian* for its continuing support; and to freelance photographer Eddie Whitham. Stan Lewandowski of the Past Players' Association has loaned important photographs and helped with the captioning of team pictures. Ernie Day, the club's unofficial historian, has offered insight and advice. Robert Gate, Alex Service and John Huxley have also given valuable assistance. Thank you, one and all.

Front cover: *Alexander the Great. Alex Murphy holds aloft the Challenge Cup after the 1974 Wembley win.*
Back cover: *Ken Kelly (top), Bill Shankland (middle) and Billy Dingsdale.*

It was a very good year: Warrington's 1933 Challenge Cup final team as they were pictured in the Wembley programme for the match against Huddersfield.

100 WARRINGTON GREATS

Jack Arkwright snr
Kevin Ashcroft
Willie Aspinall
Allan Bateman
Harry Bath
Billy Belshaw
Brian Bevan
John Bevan
Paul Bishop
Phil Blake
Alf Boardman
Jeff Bootle
Les Boyd
Brian Brady
Lee Briers
Ernie Brookes
Dave Brown
Brian Case
Jim Challinor
Bill Chapman
Dave Chisnall
Dave Cotton snr
Neil Courtney
Paul Cullen
Billy Cunliffe
Tom Cunliffe
Dai Davies
Jonathan Davies
George Dickenson
Billy Dingsdale
Des Drummond
Ronnie Duane
Bob Eccles
Jackie Edwards

Jim Featherstone
Jack Fish
Jackie Fleming
Tommy Flynn
Phil Ford
Mark Forster
Eric Fraser
Eric Frodsham
Bobby Fulton
Laurie Gilfedder
Brian Glover
Parry Gordon
Bobby Greenough
Andy Gregory
Mike Gregory
Iestyn Harris
Gerry Helme
Steve Hesford
Billy Holding
Bob Jackson
Albert Johnson
Brian Johnson
Ben Jolley
Les Jones
Ken Kelly
Billy Kirk
Bryn Knowelden
Toa Kohe-Love
Allan Langer
Dave Lyon
Greg Mackey
Duane Mann
Tommy Martyn
Stan McCormick

Jackie Melling
Gary Mercer
Jack Miller
Cec Mountford
Alex Murphy
Albert Naughton
Mike Nicholas
Derek Noonan
Terry O'Grady
Harold Palin
Alf Peacock
Lee Penny
Barry Philbin
Albert Pimblett
Ian Potter
Ray Price
Mark Roberts
Bob Ryan
Ron Ryder
Paul Sculthorpe
Charlie Seeling
Bill Shankland
Kelly Shelford
Frank Shugars
Arthur Skelhorne
Kevin Tamati
George Thomas
Tommy Thompson
Jim Tranter
Derek Whitehead
Frank Williams
John Woods

The top twenty players, who appear here in italics, occupy two pages instead of the usual one.

Jack Arkwright snr
Second-row forward, 1934-45

Season	Apps	Tries	Pts
1934/35	35	5	15
1935/36	29	4	20*
1936/37	35	4	12
1937/38	29	9	27
1938/39	28	7	21
1939/40	6	1	3
1945/46	2	0	0
TOTAL	**164**	**30**	**98**

*Arkwright also kicked 4 goals.

Jack Arkwright was one of Warrington's finest second-row forwards and holds a unique place in the annals of sport because he was sent off twice in the same game. The remarkable events unfolded during Great Britain's tour of Australia in 1936 when the Lions were playing a match against one of the tough provincial teams, Northern Districts. Years later, Arkwright recalled: 'I tackled one of their players a bit hard and another bloke burst up and jumped on me. I thumped him and the referee ordered me off. But their captain, possibly with revenge in mind, made a plea on my behalf. The referee relented. After taking more stick and with only two minutes of the match remaining, I thumped their captain. The referee spotted me. "All right," I said. "I'm going this time." And I walked.'

Three days later, Arkwright was sent off again, after laying out Australian prop-forward Ray Stehr in the third Test between the Kangaroos and Great Britain at the Sydney Cricket Ground. When, eventually, he was revived, Stehr was sent off too. Arkwright, then – all 6ft 3in and 16 stones of him – was a player you wanted on your side rather than the opposition's.

He joined Warrington from his home-town club, St Helens, in 1934 and soon became a dominant figure in the Warrington pack and at the club. In 1935, for example, he was instrumental in bringing St Helens hooker Dave Cotton to Wilderspool. He also succeeded Bill Shankland as Warrington captain in 1937.

At Wilderspool he played in three major finals, the Championship finals of 1935 and 1937 and the Challenge Cup final of 1936, but had to settle for a losers' medal on each occasion. He did, however, figure in the Warrington team that won the Lancashire Cup in October 1937.

The outbreak of the Second World War effectively brought his career to a premature end, although he did play twice for the first team at the start of 1945/46 season. But that is not the end of the Arkwright story, because his son, Jack junior, following him into the Warrington pack between 1959 and 1962 and his grandson, Chris, played for St Helens in the 1980s.

Neither could compare with Jack, however, whose career brought him 6 Great Britain caps, 4 England caps and 8 appearances for Lancashire. He died, aged eighty-seven, in January 1990.

Kevin Ashcroft
Hooker, 1972-75

Season	Apps	Tries	D/Gls	Pts
1972/73	41	13	6	51
1973/74	43	5	12	39
1974/75	39(1)	2	5	11
TOTAL	**123(1)**	**20**	**23**	**101**

Kevin Ashcroft served Warrington with great distinction as a player and as a coach. As the Warrington hooker, he scored the first try at Wembley as the Wire beat Featherstone Rovers 24-9 in May 1974 to win the Challenge Cup.

As the Warrington coach, he guided the team to a comprehensive 16-0 victory over St Helens in the 1982 Lancashire Cup final at Central Park. The following season, he masterminded Warrington's rise to third place in the Championship.

Born in Newton-le-Willows in 1944, Ashcroft began his professional career with Dewsbury and Rochdale Hornets, before linking up with Alex Murphy at Leigh in 1967. The pair then shared in Leigh's finest hour, the 1971 Challenge Cup final victory over red-hot favourites Leeds.

Five days later, Murphy took charge at Warrington but did not achieve sustained success until he signed Ashcroft for £7,000 in the summer of 1972 and made him vice-captain. 'Our supporters wanted a top-class hooker,' said Warrington chairman Ossie Davies, 'So we bought them the best. Kevin is a brilliant player and will ensure our backs see plenty of the ball.' Warrington won the League Leaders' rose bowl in 1972/73 but had no luck in the cup competitions. All that changed the following season as Warrington collected the Captain Morgan Trophy, the Player's No. 6 Trophy, the Challenge Cup and the Club Championship.

Ashcroft was the man of the match in the Player's No. 6 final, after winning the scrum battle 15-5 to supply his team-mates with plenty of possession. Typically, Ashcroft gave his £25 prize to the Wigan groundsman as a tribute to the hard work he had done on the pitch after a morning downpour.

At the end of the 1973/74 season, Ashcroft went on his second tour to Australia and collected his sixth Great Britain cap. He continued to produce international form throughout the 1974/75 season as Warrington reached two more finals, against Salford in the BBC2 Floodlit Trophy and against Widnes in the Challenge Cup. He also became the first Warrington player to kick a one-point drop goal, against Widnes in an 8-8 draw at Wilderspool, in August 1975.

The return trip to Wembley, however, was Ashcroft's last match as a Warrington player before he became Leigh's player-coach in June 1975. He linked up with Murphy again at Salford in August 1978 before becoming Warrington coach in November 1982. These days he is the commercial manager at Leigh, but rightly remains a popular figure at all the clubs he has been associated with.

Willie Aspinall
Stand-off, 1962-71

Season	Apps	Tries	Pts
1961/62	2	0	0
1962/63	14	4	12
1963/64	18	3	9
1964/65	41	9	27
1965/66	39(1)	4	12
1966/67	32	10	30
1967/68	20(1)	9	27
1968/69	33	2	6
1969/70	29(3)	8	24
1970/71	35	6	18
TOTAL	**263(5)**	**55**	**165**

Aspinall also kicked 40 goals and 30 drop goals.

Willie Aspinall was one of the successes of Great Britain's tour to Australia and New Zealand in the summer of 1966. Aspinall, who was the Warrington captain at the time and the club's only tourist, played in 20 matches on the trip, scoring 10 tries. He also collected his only international cap with a try-scoring display at Auckland's Carlaw Park as Great Britain beat New Zealand 22-14 to take the series 2-0.

Aspinall had joined Warrington from the UGB (United Glassblowers) junior club in St Helens and made his debut at Widnes on Good Friday 1962. Jackie Edwards and Bobby Greenough were the first-choice halfbacks at the time and so Aspinall – who weighed in at 5ft 9in and 11st 7lb – had to be patient and turn out on the wing when it was required.

By the start of the 1964/65 season, however, he was the number one stand-off at the club and would remain so for the next seven seasons before he moved on to Rochdale Hornets. At Leeds, on the opening day of the 1964/65 season, Aspinall unwittingly made a little bit of Warrington history when, after 21 minutes, he became the first Wire player to be substituted when he was replaced by Joe Pickavance. Substitutions were a new innovation that season, but were only allowed up to half-time and then only if a player was injured.

Despite his length of service, Aspinall only collected two winners' medals while he was at Wilderspool – for the Lancashire Cup win over Rochdale in 1965 and for the Lancashire League title success in 1968.

He was, however, a drop goal expert and his career total of 30 puts him in third place in the club's all-time list, behind Steve Hesford (47) and Paul Bishop (42). Aspinall also made 7 appearances for Lancashire between 1965 and 1967, scoring 2 tries.

He was in the Rochdale side that lost 27-16 to Warrington in the 1974 Player's No.6 Trophy final at Central Park.

'I had a lot of time for his ability and his professionalism,' said Warrington teammate Jackie Melling. 'He was a good professional and a talented player.'

Allan Bateman
Centre, 1990-95

Season	Apps	Tries	Pts
1990/91	28(1)	9	36
1991/92	22(1)	5	20
1992/93	30(1)	11	44
1993/94	30	10	41*
1994/95	28(1)	17	68
TOTAL	138(4)	52	209

*Bateman also kicked a drop goal.

Allan Bateman was the last great player to join Warrington directly from Welsh rugby union – Jonathan Davies was signed later, but he came via Widnes, whereas Bateman moved straight from Neath.

The deal was done in September 1990 with Bateman, who was twenty-five years old, reportedly agreeing a five-year contract worth £100,000. Forward Rowland Phillips, Bateman's Neath and Wales team-mate, signed on the same day on similar terms but never quite made the grade. Bateman, on the other hand, was an almost instant success, scoring four tries against Runcorn Highfield in the Regal Trophy in only his seventh full first-team appearance.

Bateman is best remembered for his cast-iron defence, however, which is why his centre partnership with Davies was such a success. Bateman, at 5ft 10in and 12st 7lb, never missed a tackle while Davies could be relied upon to produce the occasional flash of genius. 'I don't really set myself goals at the start of the season,' said Bateman, 'but I set myself the same goal before every match – not to miss any tackles.'

While at Wilderspool, Bateman won 3 Great Britain caps, coming on as a substitute for Davies in the first Test against Australia at Wembley in October 1994 and helping to secure a famous 8-4 victory. He also made 11 appearances for the reborn Welsh side, scoring 5 tries.

Just four months after switching codes, in January 1991 Bateman was a member of the Warrington team who lifted the Regal Trophy by beating Bradford Northern 12-2 in the final at Headingley. He was also a member of the side who were crushed 40-10 by Wigan in the final of the same competition at Huddersfield's McAlpine Stadium four years later.

After leaving Warrington, 'Batman' played for the Australian side Cronulla – where he was known as 'The Clamp' because of his tremendous defensive qualities – before returning to rugby union with Richmond, followed by Northampton and then back to Neath. Before joining Warrington, he had won 4 caps for Wales and by the end of last year had taken that tally to 35 (with 10 tries). His autobiography, *There and Back Again*, caused a stir in the Valleys when he said he had been offered £5,000 to 'throw' a Five Nations match against Ireland in 1990.

Harry Bath
Second row forward, 1948-57

Season	Apps	Tries	Goals	Pts
1947/48	10	6	2	22
1948/49	45	16	10	68
1949/50	36	14	7	56
1950/51	40	10	59	148
1951/52	27	6	70	158
1952/53	40	13	162	363
1953/54	45	4	153	318
1954/55	35	8	118	260
1955/56	42	12	154	344
1956/57	26	1	77	157
TOTAL	**346**	**90**	**812**	**1894**

Australian forward Harry Bath was the first overseas captain to lift the Challenge Cup, for Warrington at Wembley in 1950. He was also a vital component of the Warrington team that completed the impressive League and Cup double in 1953/54, contributing more than 300 points to the cause and kicking goals in all the important matches.

Bath had come to England from Balmain to play for Barrow, but he did not settle in Cumbria and jumped at the chance to join Warrington in March 1948. By the time he returned home to Australia in 1957, he was the most prolific try-scoring forward, most prolific points scorer and second greatest goalkicker in the club's history. Even now, almost half a century later, he still holds one club record, for scoring 363 points in the 1952/53 season.

Bath, who was 5ft 11in and 14st 7lb, played most of his career in the second row, although he could, and did, perform admirably at prop. He was not an eighty-minute player, like his second-row partner Bob Ryan, and Bath tended to pace himself, lulling the opposition into complacency before coming into a move with such devastating effect that he was over the try-line before they knew what had hit them. In short, he was world class and he and his Warrington team-mate Brian Bevan were perhaps the two best Australian players never to have worn the Green and Gold of the national side.

Bath needed to have a pain-killing injection before the 1950 Challenge Cup final against Widnes, but that did not stop him scoring a typical try in the first half when he crashed through a quartet of would-be tacklers. He had signed too late to be eligible for the Championship play-offs of 1948, when Warrington won the title for the first time, and then had to suffer Championship final defeats against Huddersfield in 1949 and Workington Town in 1951.

Everything fell into place in the 1953/54 season, however, as Bath's two goals against Halifax at Wembley set up the Challenge Cup final replay at Odsal Stadium which Warrington won 8-4 in front of a world record crowd of 102,569.

He also kicked the four goals that gave Warrington an 8-7 victory over Halifax in the Championship final at Maine Road to seal the double. Twelve months later, his two goals were what made the difference between

Cup king: Warrington captain Harry Bath is carried shoulder high by Bill Derbyshire (left) and Ike Fishwick (right) on a lap of honour at Wembley in 1950 with Les Jones and Bryn Knowelden.

Warrington and Oldham as the Wire proved their mettle by retaining the title.

Bath played his final game for Warrington against Bramley at Wilderspool in February 1957 before returning to Australia for three great seasons with Sydney St George. When he finished playing, he took up coaching with just as much success. In 1968 and 1970, he masterminded Australia's World Cup wins and in 1977 and 1979 he coached Sydney St George to Grand Final triumphs over Parramatta and Canterbury respectively.

The St George full-back in that second triumph was future Warrington coach Brian Johnson. 'He signed me for St George when I was twenty-two and was the coach for my first three seasons,' Johnson recalled. 'He had a very good record as a coach in Australia. He was very clever ... I guess he was the last of the old-style coaches but he wasn't a yeller, a shouter and a screamer. He was particularly good with the forwards, but I learned a lot from him too, in terms of how to back up and when to back up. He was a great bloke.'

Bath is now in his late seventies and his health is failing, but he is still a much-respected figure in his homeland – where he is affectionately known as 'The Old Fox'. In 1999, he was invited to the official opening of Stadium Australia in Sydney. Later that year, more than 500 supporters packed into the St George Club to pay tribute to their former player and coach.

Billy Belshaw
Full-back, centre and stand-off, 1937-46

Season	Apps	Tries	Goals	Pts
1937/38	24	4	19	50
1938/39	41	3	45	99
1939/40	26	6	50	118
1940/41	15	11	27	87
1945/46	26	5	27	69
TOTAL	132	29	168	423

Belshaw also kicked 5 drop goals.

Warrington have twice broken the world transfer record. The last time was in November 1949, when they paid £4,600 for Widnes centre Albert Naughton. The first time was in October 1937, when they splashed out £1,450 for the Liverpool Stanley full-back Billy Belshaw.

As you would expect, Belshaw was an established Great Britain international, although Warrington were sadly robbed of some of his best years by the Second World War. Belshaw had toured Australia and New Zealand with the 1936 Lions and actually joined the Wire part-way through the Ashes series of 1937. He played in all three Tests; the first as a Liverpool Stanley player and the second two while with Warrington. Great Britain won the series 2-1.

Belshaw could score tries, kick goals and drop goals. He was also a very versatile and reliable player and appeared at full-back, stand-off and in both centre positions during the 1938/39 season – the last before the outbreak of war.

He continued to play for Warrington in the Emergency League and took part in the famous match against Broughton Rangers in September 1940 when a German aircraft attacked the Thames Board Mills factory at Arpley Meadows, less than a mile from Wilderspool. The ground was later requisitioned by the Army and used as a storage depot and so Belshaw represented Huddersfield and, later, Wigan as a guest player. His spell at Central Park was particularly successful and he was an important member of the Wigan team who won the Championship by beating Dewsbury in both legs of the final in 1944.

Billy Belshaw was the Warrington captain for the first post-war season and was playing at full-back when an unknown Australian named Brian Bevan made his debut on the right wing against Oldham that November. Belshaw's best days were behind him, however, and he was transferred to Bramley in 1946.

A world record transfer fee of £1,450 seems laughable today, but inflation means that Belshaw would have been worth 100 times that amount in the present climate.

Brian Bevan
Winger, 1945-62

Season	Apps	Tries	Pts
1945/46	1	0	0
1946/47	42	48	212*
1947/48	43	57	171
1948/49	44	56	168
1949/50	39	30	90
1950/51	40	60	180
1951/52	39	46	138
1952/53	41	66	198
1953/54	45	62	186
1954/55	37	61	183
1955/56	41	53	159
1956/57	26	14	42
1957/58	40	45	135
1958/59	40	54	162
1959/60	40	40	120
1960/61	42	35	105
1961/62	20	13	39
TOTAL	**620**	**740**	**2288**

*Bevan also kicked 34 goals.

Warrington winger Brian Bevan is so far ahead of his rivals that his records will never be broken. From his debut in 1945 until his final appearance in 1964, Bevan scored a world record 796 tries, including 740 for Warrington. Billy Boston, his nearest rival, scored 571 tries for Wigan, Blackpool Borough and Great Britain. Martin Offiah celebrated his 500th touchdown last year. The rest are nowhere. Bony and bandaged, Leeds did not take a second glance at Bevan when he turned up at Headingley for a trial in 1945. Bill Shankland, the former Warrington captain, then suggested that Bevan try his luck at Wilderspool. The rest is history.

Bevan played for Warrington's A team against Widnes A at Wilderspool on 10 November 1945 and astonished the small crowd with his pace, scoring a brilliant try from halfway a minute from time. Seven days later, he made his first-team debut at home to Oldham and although he did not score a try, Warrington could not wait to sign him. Bevan had to return to Australia to be demobbed, but promised to return to England to play for Warrington the following season. He became the shining light of Warrington's most successful era. With him in the side, Warrington won the Championship three times (1947/48, 1953/54 and 1954/55), the Challenge Cup twice (1949/50 and 1953/54) and the Lancashire Cup once (1959/60).

Bevan was Warrington's leading try-scorer every season from 1946/47 to 1960/61, except for the 1956/57 campaign when he was plagued by injuries. He scored tries against every other club and against the touring Kangaroos and Kiwis. But statistics alone cannot convey the excitement that Bevan was able to generate in the massive crowds which turned out to watch him.

Bevan was born in Sydney on 24 June 1924. As a small boy he spent hours on Bondi Beach, surfing, swimming and developing a seemingly frail body into an athletic frame. When he first played rugby at school he was a stand-off but he fractured an elbow in one game and his father, Rick, who had played for Eastern Suburbs during the 1920s, advised him to move out to the wing.

Mud lark: Brian Bevan skates across a heavy pitch towards the try line.

Bevan scored his first try for Warrington against Salford at Wilderspool in the first round of the Lancashire Cup in September 1946. Tries followed at regular intervals thereafter. His best haul was a club record seven in one match, which he achieved against Leigh at Wilderspool on Easter Monday 1948. He repeated the feat against Bramley at Wilderspool five years later. He also scored six tries in a match four times and five tries in a match on six occasions.

As well as scoring tries in remarkable quantities, he also scored tries of remarkable quality. At Oldham in the second round of the Challenge Cup in March 1954, Warrington were trailing 4-2 and on their way out of the competition until Bevan intercepted a pass on his own 25-yard line and raced away for a match-winning score. Warrington went on to win the cup and do the double. His best try, however, is believed to have come at Wigan's Central Park in the Wardonia Cup pre-season game in August 1948, when he received the ball behind his own try line and set off on a breathtaking diagonal run to score in the opposite corner less than ten seconds later.

Bevan's final appearance for Warrington was against Leigh at Wilderspool on Easter Monday 1962, when more than 16,000 supporters turned out to bid him farewell. Sure enough, Bevan signed off with a try, his 740th for Warrington and his 464th at Wilderspool. As the final whistle sounded, supporters surged on to the pitch and Bevan was carried shoulder high by his teammates and finally left the field through a guard of honour of applauding Leigh players. Minutes later, Bevan appeared in the main stand as the crowd sang 'For he's a jolly good fellow' and 'Waltzing Matilda'. Bevan went on to play for Blackpool Borough for two seasons, before finally hanging up his boots at the age of thirty-nine.

When, in October 1988, the RFL instituted a Hall of Fame, Bevan was one of the founder members and when he died, aged sixty-six, in June 1991 a generation of rugby league fans went into mourning. Two years later, a magnificent statue of Bevan in full flight was officially unveiled on the Wilderspool Causeway roundabout to make sure his heroic deeds on the rugby fields of England will never be forgotten.

John Bevan
Winger/centre, 1973-86

Season	Apps	Tries	Pts
1973/74	35	22	66
1974/75	37	29	87
1975/76	31	18	54
1976/77	23	17	51
1977/78	39	30	90
1978/79	23	17	51
1979/80	34	25	75
1980/81	38	19	57
1981/82	28	5	15
1982/83	14	7	21
1983/84	19(1)	10	40
1984/85	8	2	8
1985/86	2	0	0
TOTAL	**331(1)**	**201**	**615**

John Bevan also kicked 6 goals and a drop goal.

John Bevan was the swashbuckling hero for a generation of Warrington fans who started watching the Wire in the 1970s. From his debut against Castleford in September 1973 until his last appearance against Oldham in February 1986, Bevan could usually be relied upon to score a match-winning try or make a match-saving tackle and he always looked like he was enjoying himself.

The ultimate symbol of his job satisfaction, however, was the clenched-fist salute with which he celebrated his tries, starting at Leigh on Boxing Day 1973. 'I intercepted a ball on the halfway line and no-one was in front of me,' Bevan recalled in his testimonial brochure ten years later. 'I realised I was going to score for the first time in ages and out of frustration came delight. Up went the arm.' It became his trademark and the fans loved it, although player-coach Alex Murphy vowed he would chop the arm off if the salute ever caused him to drop the ball in the act of scoring. Thankfully, it never did.

Bevan scored four tries that Boxing Day afternoon to signal his arrival as a genuine rugby league player after just thirteen weeks in his new code. The following six months were the stuff of fairytales, with Bevan collecting four winners' medals (Captain Morgan Trophy, Player's No. 6 Trophy, Challenge Cup and Club Championship), playing at Wembley, being selected for the tour of Australia and New Zealand and winning the first of his 6 Great Britain caps.

The 1974/75 season was almost as good, with Bevan scoring a try at Wembley in the opening minutes of the Challenge Cup final defeat against Widnes and making the first of 17 appearances for the reborn Welsh national side. It was too good to last, however, and it took Bevan another eight years to earn his next four winners' medals (two for John Player Trophy successes and two for Lancashire Cup wins), although the tries and the memories kept piling up.

As the seasons rolled by, Bevan was increasingly used as a centre, a loose-forward and even a stand-off. His speed and, in particular, his strength made him a formidable opponent anywhere. At St Helens in

Flying machine: John Bevan scores in the corner during the Challenge Cup second round tie at Wigan in February 1975. Wigan full-back Bill Francis is the player giving chase. Warrington won 24-17.

September 1979, for example, Bevan began the match on the left wing and was switched to the loose-forward slot after Warrington had stand-off Ken Kelly sent off and lost prop Steve Hogan and No. 13 Mike Peers with injuries. Bevan finished the afternoon with four tries and winning pay. 'Sleeves rolled up, socks down to his ankles, Bevan looked more like one of the Bash Street Kids and caused mayhem wherever he went,' wrote Robert Gate in *Gone North – Volume II*. 'Muscular, bursting with power and energy, Bevan simply epitomised aggression and determination.'

Those qualities had already seen Bevan play on the wing for Cardiff, Wales, the British Lions and the Barbarians before he joined Warrington in September 1973, one month short of his twenty-third birthday.

Best of all for Wire fans, in November 1972, Bevan had rejected the chance to join Wigan – a Warrington hero indeed.

'I was extremely lucky,' said Bevan, modestly. 'When I first decided to play Rugby League, I had never been to the north-west and didn't know anything about the area. A few clubs were interested in signing me, but I went for Warrington and it turned out to be a tremendous place. I was aware of Brian Bevan's reputation and knew it could have gone against me if I'd had a bad start at the club, but the spectators took to me stright away and always made me feel incredibly welcome.'

Paul Bishop
Half-back, 1984-90

Season	Apps	Tries	Goals	Pts
1984/85	2(1)	1	7	18
1985/86	21(3)	13	63	191
1986/87	34(3)	12	99	263
1988/89	19(2)	6	0	26
1989/90	16(2)	2	6	30
1990/91	10	4	8	32
TOTAL	102(11)	38	183	560

Bishop also kicked 42 drop goals.

On his day, Paul Bishop was one of the best half-backs in the business. One such day was the Premiership Trophy semi-final against Wigan at Central Park in 1986, when he kicked a club record five drop goals as Warrington scored a famous 23-12 victory.

He kicked one in the first half and four in the second and each was like a stake through the Wigan heart. Bishop also scored a try and kicked three goals that May afternoon for a 15-point haul – he virtually beat Wigan on his own. Bishop was again among the points in the final with a try and five goals as Warrington thrashed Halifax 38-10 at Elland Road.

Bishop, the son of former Great Britain scrum-half Tommy Bishop, had joined Warrington from the Thatto Heath amateur club in St Helens in July 1984 and made a sensational first-team debut at Wilderspool just three months later. Still only seventeen, he scored a try and kicked seven goals as Warrington beat Workington Town 42-30. However, his second full appearance – at Wilderspool the following month – almost ended in tragedy. Bishop, just 5ft 7in and 12 st, was on the receiving end of a hard, but fair, tackle from Oldham winger Green Vigo and swallowed his tongue. The youngster started having convulsions, but physiotherapist Gordon Pinkney, helped by coaches Derek Whitehead and Tony Barrow, managed to release the tongue and save his life.

Bishop did not play again for the first team that season, but was one of the mainstays of the side in 1985/86 and 1986/87, making 2 appearances for the Great Britain Under-21s against France in March 1987. At the end of that season he joined the Cronulla club in Sydney, but returned for a second spell at Wilderspool in 1988. The highlight this time was the 1990 Challenge Cup final against Wigan at Wembley.

Bishop began nervously, missing two penalty kicks at goal, before hitting the target twice to make the half-time score 16-8. After 61 minutes, however, his growing influence on the game was halted by a thundering tackle from Joe Lydon and he was substituted with concussion.

Just seven months after the final, Bishop was given a free transfer after criticising the club in the press. He joined St Helens a few days later and played for them in the 1991 Challenge Cup final against Wigan before moving on to Halifax.

Phil Blake
Centre or stand-off, 1985-86, 1988-89

Season	Apps	Tries	D/Gls	Pts
1985/86	19	22	1	89
1988/89	25	19	3	79
TOTAL	**44**	**41**	**4**	**168**

Australian centre or stand-off Phil Blake was Warrington's first ever video star. After the 'Manly Wonderboy' was signed in the summer of 1985, the Touchdown Club at Wilderspool was proud to present video footage of his try-scoring exploits back at home. Blake looked like a gifted and brilliant attacking player, and so it proved. He was never too interested in the defensive side of the game – Les Boyd once replayed a recording of a Blake tackle over and over again at a training session, almost in disbelief – but when it came to spotting openings and scoring tries he had few equals.

During his first spell with the club, he operated primarily as a centre. When he returned three years later as a South Sydney player he was mainly used as a half-back. One thing remained constant, however, his ability to score tries. In both his seasons at Wilderspool, Blake was the leading try-scorer – despite arriving late and leaving early because of his contractual commitments in Australia.

Blake signalled his intentions from day one, scoring two tries on his debut against Workington Town in the second round of the Lancashire Cup. In the semi-final against Widnes he scored the match-winning try, having previously set up the opener for Andy Gregory. In his next match, against Salford at Wilderspool in the Slalom Lager Championship, he scored four tries and a drop goal to inspire a 41-19 victory. He was injured in the opening minutes of the Lancashire Cup final defeat against Wigan at Knowsley Road but quickly returned to fitness and form.

Blake was even more influential during his second spell with the club and his last appearance for Warrington, at Hull Kingston Rovers in the quarter-final of the Challenge Cup, was one of his best ever. Blake was comfortably the man of the match after creating all but one of Warrington's five tries in a 30-4 victory. Warrington asked if Blake could return to England for the semi-final against Wigan, but South Sydney refused. It is no exaggeration to say that his formidable presence could have made all the difference in such a tight contest – Wigan won 13-6.

Wigan certainly respected Blake and signed him on a short-term contract the following season. He played just 11 games for the Central Park club, scoring 7 tries and kicking 17 goals. It is almost frightening to think that Blake, despite all his gifts, was never considered good enough to play for Australia.

Alf Boardman
Forward, 1898-1914

Season	Apps	Tries	Pts
1898/99	23	0	0
1899/00	29	0	0
1900/01	34	0	0
1901/02	27	0	0
1902/03	29	0	0
1903/04	35	2	6
1904/05	31	3	9
1905/06	34	0	0
1906/07	36	8	24
1907/08	28	2	6
1908/09	34	9	27
1909/10	35	3	9
1910/11	25	1	3
1911/12	2	1	3
1912/13	0	0	0
1913/14	1	0	0
TOTAL	**403**	**29**	**87**

Alf Boardman was the first Warrington player to make 400 appearances for the first team, including the club's first four Challenge Cup finals.

He joined Warrington from Latchford Rangers and made his debut at home to Swinton on Saturday 3 September 1898, when the Wirepullers, as they were known, played at Wilderspool for the very first time.

Boardman soon established himself in the pack and was an automatic choice when Warrington reached their first Challenge Cup final, against Batley at Headingley in April 1901. Warrington lost 6-0 and were beaten in the final again three years later by Halifax, despite Boardman being acclaimed in newspaper reports as the best forward on the pitch. It was a case of third time lucky for Boardman, however, when Hull Kingston Rovers were defeated 6-0 at Headingley in the 1905 final and he finally got his hands on a winners' medal.

Forward play in those days, in rugby league and rugby union, required players to maraud, dribble and scrummage and Boardman, who was 5ft 10in and 14st 4lb, was quite happy to do all three for the good of the team. In 1906/07, rugby league changed forever when it was reduced to a thirteen-a-side game, but Boardman was quickly able to adapt and collected his second Challenge Cup winners' medal in April 1907 when Oldham were outclassed 17-3 in the final at Wheater's Field, Broughton.

He continued to be a first-team regular until the end of the 1910/11 season, after which he turned out for the A team. In his prime, Boardman won a single England cap in 1905 and made 6 appearances for Lancashire. His younger brother, Peter, followed him into the Warrington pack from 1907 to 1912, making 64 appearances.

Alf Boardman also played in the first Warrington team to wear numbers on their jerseys – against Leigh at Wilderspool for a Lancashire Cup second round tie on Saturday 28 October 1905. However, the innovation did not bring Warrington any luck as they lost 5-2 in front of 6,000 fans.

Jeff Bootle
Full-back and winger, 1964-69

Season	Apps	Tries	Goals	Pts
1963/64	14	11	10	53
1964/65	42	12	93	222
1965/66	40	5	78	171
1966/67	21(4)	6	16	50
1967/68	8	1	23	49
1968/69	40(2)	7	125	271
TOTAL	**165(6)**	**42**	**345**	**816**

12 of Bootle's goals were drop goals.

These days, opposition fans would no doubt taunt Jeff Bootle as a 'Wigan reject' because of his transfer from Central Park to Wilderspool for a fee of £2,500 – but there was definitely nothing second rate about this most versatile of players.

Bootle played on the wing, in the centres and later at loose-forward and in the second row for Warrington, but is perhaps best remembered as a goalkicking full-back. His finest hour was probably the 1965 Lancashire Cup final against Rochdale Hornets at Knowsley Road, when he captained the side from the full-back position and kicked two goals in a 16-5 victory played out before 21,000 fans.

It was the first Lancashire Cup final to be played under floodlights, and the full Warrington team were: Bootle; Ray Fisher, Jow Pickavance, Jackie Melling, Brian Glover; Willie Aspinall, John Smith; Bill Payne, Geoff Oakes, Charlie Winslade, Geoff Robinson, Mal Thomas and Billy Hayes. Melling (2) and Glover were the try-scorers.

Two weeks later, in a perfect illustration of the topsy-turvy nature of sport, Bootle was stripped of the captaincy after he refused to play against his former club because he had been selected on the wing. That minor dispute was quickly settled, however, and he went on to give four more years of sterling service before retiring, at the early age of just twenty-nine, in the summer of 1969 citing business reasons.

In his final season, Bootle, who was 6ft tall and weighed 13st 10lb, had joined that elite group of goal-kickers by registering a century of goals, including nine in one memorable match against Doncaster at Wilderspool in November 1968.

At Wigan, Bootle had scored 27 tries and kicked 27 goals in 65 appearances made between 1958 and 1963, including the 1961 Challenge Cup final defeat against St Helens at Wembley, when he played at left centre.

Les Boyd
Prop-forward, 1985-89

Season	Apps	Tries	Pts
1985/86	33	13	52
1986/87	26	5	20
1987/88	10(2)	2	8
1988/89	15	0	0
TOTAL	**84(2)**	**20**	**80**

In 1998, Warrington Guardian readers were asked to compile their all-time favourite Warrington teams in a poll to mark Wilderspool's centenary match. The player with the most votes was not Brian Bevan, the club's world record try-scorer, but another Australian, the bruising prop-forward Les Boyd.

Bob Eccles, one of Warrington's greatest second-row forwards, telephoned Boyd to tell him the good news but miscalculated the time difference between England and Australia and awoke the sleeping giant in the middle of the night. Boyd, however, laughed off the mistake with the grace and style of a true champion. Sir Les Boyd, as he was affectionately known by Warrington fans, was not always such a gentleman on the pitch however.

Boyd was representing New South Wales in the opening State of Origin match of 1983, when his tackle on Darryl Brahman shattered the Queenslander's jaw. The referee saw nothing wrong with the big hit but after officials studied a video recording of the incident they banned Boyd for a year.

Boyd's comeback in 1984 lasted just three matches before he was cited for gouging and received a fifteen-month ban, effectively ending his Sydney career. Still, English clubs were desperate to sign him as his second suspension drew to a close and Warrington were lucky enough to win the race. By now, Boyd was twenty-eight and, by and large, a reformed character – although still a player who would never take a backwards step.

Boyd made his debut in the second row in a Lancashire Cup semi-final against Widnes at Wilderspool in October 1985, but soon made the No. 8 jersey, and the captaincy, his own. The front row of Les Boyd, Kevin Tamati and Bob Jackson became the most feared in the club's history.

Boyd's finest hour in a Warrington jersey was undoubtedly the 1986 Premiership final against Halifax at Elland Road, when he led the Wire to a famous 38-10 victory. For a big man – Boyd weighed 16st – he had a surprising turn of pace and scored two tries that May afternoon to claim the Harry Sunderland Trophy as the man of the match. Boyd continued that rampaging form at the start of the 1986/87 season. In the semi-final of the John Player Special Trophy, for example, Boyd tamed Kurt Sorensen of Widnes, a mighty Kiwi forward, as Warrington scored a spectacular 35-4 victory.

Calm down: Warrington's Les Boyd tries to reason with referee John Holdsworth.

Injuries, however, began to disrupt his career, causing him to miss the 1987 Premiership final against Wigan at Old Trafford. Worse was to follow when he suffered a broken arm at Halifax in only the second game of the 1987/88 season. Typically, he was back in the heart of the action against Wigan on New Year's Day 1988 in the match which Warrington coach Tony Barrow later described as 'World War Three'. The game exploded into a brawl as early as the ninth minute following a clash between Boyd and Shaun Edwards. Newspaper pictures also showed the rugged Aussie launching a haymaker at his former team-mate, the Wigan scrum-half Andy Gregory. He was sent to the sin-bin for his indiscretions.

When Boyd suffered a second broken arm against St Helens at Wilderspool in the second round of the Challenge Cup in February 1988, it seemed that a career which had earned him 19 international caps was finally over for good.

However, new Warrington coach Brian Johnson and chairman Peter Higham persuaded him to return to Wilderspool in January 1989 for one last hurrah. Boyd's presence re-energised the fans and seemed to bring the best out of Warrington's other Australian prop that season, Steve Roach. With the two of them bossing the forward battle, the Wire built up a 6-4 lead over Wigan in the Challenge Cup semi-final at Maine Road before Joe Lydon levelled the scores with a penalty goal and then broke Warrington hearts with a record-breaking, 61-yard drop goal.

Les Boyd pulled on a primrose and blue jersey for the final time in the American Challenge match against Wigan in Milwaukee in June 1989 before returning to Australia. He paid a flying visit to England in August 2001 to mark the fifteenth anniversary of that Premiership Trophy success. The passing years and the painful injuries had taken their toll, but Boyd clearly remained a Warrington legend.

Brian Brady
Prop-forward, 1965-75

Season	Apps	Tries	Pts
1964/65	0(1)	0	0
1965/66	4(2)	0	0
1966/67	39	2	6
1967/68	36	5	15
1968/69	36	7	21
1969/70	37	8	24
1970/71	15(5)	0	0
1971/72	37	13	39
1972/73	30(3)	10	30
1973/74	42(1)	9	27
1974/75	23(5)	0	0
1975/76	10(2)	0	0
TOTAL	**309(19)**	**54**	**162**

Brian Brady's enormous strength earned him the nickname 'Bully' and the respect of team-mates and opponents alike. At 5ft 11in and 15st 7lb, Brady was ideally built for life as a prop-forward and 50 of his 54 tries came from that position – a club record.

Brady usually operated on the blind-side of the front row and was a robust, no-nonsense forward, although a fair one. In twelve seasons at Warrington, his only club, he was never sent off.

Brady was a lad from Wigan who joined Warrington as a teenager and graduated through the club's Colts side. He made his first-team debut as a substitute at Wakefield, aged eighteen, on the last day of the 1964/65 season and was a regular in the side two years later.

However, he had to wait until his testimonial season, 1973/74, to enjoy the kind of success he really deserved. Warrington won four major competitions that season – the Captain Morgan Trophy, the Player's No. 6 Trophy, the Club Championship and the Challenge Cup – and Brady played in all four finals.

Sadly, at Wembley, Brady had to leave the field after 17 minutes to have stitches in a head wound, but returned to the fray four minutes from time to replace the injured Mike Nicholas. Seven days later, he was able to play a more prominent part when he crashed over for the opening try against St Helens in the Club Championship final.

Brady, who worked as a welder, was under no romantic illusions about the life of a professional sportsman and the role of a prop-forward. After a surprise win at Leeds, he was asked to account for the vast improvement in the team's performance. 'Pound notes,' he replied, in his best Wigan accent. His testimonial year, incidentally, raised £2,000 – a fine sum for a deserving player.

Brady also made 5 appearances for Lancashire between 1967 and 1974. His brother Jim, a scrum-half, played 11 times for Warrington in 1970 and 1971 before moving on to Swinton.

Lee Briers
Half-back, 1997-present

Season	Apps	Tries	Goals	Pts
1997	22	4	45	112
1998	22	4	49	119
1999	32(1)	6	83	196
2000	23(9)	17	93	255
2001	25(2)	12	86	224
TOTAL	**124(12)**	**43**	**356**	**906**

Briers has also kicked 22 drop goals.

The bigger the occasion, the better Lee Briers plays – without ever seeming to get the rewards he deserves. Cup semi-finals and international matches, however, are a speciality with the big stage allowing him to parade his pace, his eye for an opening and his kicking skills.

The biggest game of his career, so far, was the World Cup semi-final between underdogs Wales and world champions Australia at Huddersfield in November 2000 and Briers was the man of the match. He scored a spectacular try under the posts from an Iestyn Harris up-and-under and kicked two drop goals as Wales stunned the Kangaroos by building up a 20-8 lead after 27 minutes. Australia, of course, fought back, and won 46-22.

The following August, Briers played even better, inspiring Wales into a 16-0 lead against England at Wrexham before England hit back to win 42-33. Briers finished that game with a try, four goals and a drop goal and yet another man of the match award.

Briers has also played in three Challenge Cup semi-finals – one for St Helens and two for Warrington – accumulating another 38 points in front of the television cameras. The first of those semi-finals, for St Helens, proved to be the turning point of his career. Briers kicked six goals in a 50-20 victory over Salford but was still dropped after regular scrum-half Bobbie Goulding had completed a suspension. Briers, still only eighteen, decided he had to move on and became Warrington coach Darryl Van de Velde's first signing for a reported £65,000 in April 1997.

Briers quickly established himself as the number one goalkicker and most creative player at Wilderspool and a string of fine performances followed. In February 2000, for example, Briers smashed a long-standing club record by scoring 40 points in a match (three tries and 14 goals) in a Challenge Cup tie against York. The 2001 Challenge Cup semi-final against Bradford Bulls was another personal triumph as Briers scored three tries and kicked three goals – only to end up on the losing side.

Later that year he turned down a lucrative move to Welsh rugby union and was rewarded with his first Great Britain cap against France. Inevitably, he marked the occasion with a try.

Ernie Brookes
Stand-off, 1902-20

Season	Apps	Tries	Pts
1902/03	6	0	0
1903/04	4	0	0
1904/05	25	4	12
1905/06	27	1	3
1906/07	35	26	78
1907/08	30	11	33
1908/09	24	6	18
1909/10	30	6	18
1910/11	24	9	27
1911/12	21	1	3
1912/13	22	8	24
1913/14	16	1	3
1914/15	24	8	24
1918/19	5	0	0
1919/20	4	0	0
TOTAL	**297**	**81**	**243**

Brookes also kicked 25 goals.

When Ernie Brookes joined Warrington in May 1902, his signing-on fee was a small lemonade, a cigar and a pat on the back. Many more pats on the back followed as his strength and speed made him a first-choice for Warrington for eleven seasons and earned him 3 Great Britain caps, an England cap and 7 appearances for Lancashire.

Brookes played in the first Anglo-Australian Test match at Park Royal, London on 12 December 1908, scoring a try and kicking a controversial last-minute penalty to earn the Northern Union a well-deserved 22-22 draw. He also kept his place for the next two Tests, at St James' Park, Newcastle, and Villa Park, Birmingham – both of which Great Britain won to take the first Ashes series 2-0.

Brookes was born in Warrington in 1884 and joined the Wirepullers, as they were known, from the Bewsey junior club. He collected a Challenge Cup winners' medal against Hull Kingston Rovers in April 1905, but did not really come into his own until the 1906/07 season, when rugby league was turned into a thirteen-a-side game instead of a fifteen-a-side one. Brookes, 5ft 8in and 11st 8lb, revelled in the extra space.

Warrington also devised a tactic to bring the best out of him. Brookes would start on the left wing before exchanging places with the stand-off at half-time, to devastating effect. They even used the ploy in the 1907 Challenge Cup final against Oldham and it helped to turn a narrow advantage at the interval into a comfortable 17-3 victory.

Brookes was also a great servant to the club and was appointed captain for the 1914/15 season, before spending three years as a gunner in France in the Royal Garrison Artillery during the First World War. He made his final appearance for Warrington as an emergency scrum-half at Salford in March 1920.

A kind, shy and reserved man, Brookes died from lung cancer, aged fifty-six, in July 1940, having run the Gladstone Arms pub in Church Street for thirty years.

Dave Brown
Centre, 1937-39

Season	Apps	Tries	Goals	Pts
1936/37	21	10	10	50
1937/38	42	20	36	132
1938/39	30	18	45	144
TOTAL	93	48	91	326

Australian Dave Brown was known as 'the Don Bradman of rugby league' in Sydney because of his phenomenal points-scoring achievements. It is easy to see why.

On the 1933/34 Kangaroos tour of Great Britain, Brown, who was still only twenty, kicked 114 goals and accumulated 285 points, two records which still stand. With his club, Eastern Suburbs, he scored 35 tries in a season and 45 points in a match, two further records.

In 1936, at the tender age of 23 years 86 days, he became his country's youngest captain and celebrated by scoring two tries and kicking four goals as the Kangaroos beat Great Britain 24-8 in the first Test at the Sydney Cricket Ground. The attendance was 63,920.

Not surprisingly then, when Warrington signed him on a four-year contract in 1937, they had to make him the highest paid player in the game. Brown received a £1,000 signing-on fee plus £3-a-week and £6-a-match. Brown cut an unmistakable figure. A childhood illness had left him prematurely bald and so, uniquely among backs at the time, he chose to wear a skull cap. He stood out in other ways too.

As well as a deceptive change of pace and an eye for an opening, Brown was also a remarkable tackler, who would regularly bring forwards crashing down, and a gutsy competitor. In the 1937 Championship semi-final against Leeds at Wilderspool, for example, Brown was concussed in the opening minutes but, in the days before substitutes were allowed, he bravely carried on playing. In the dressing room after the match – which Warrington won 12-2 – the only thing Brown could remember was shaking hands with one of the Leeds players before the kick-off. He could not even remember the goal kick he attempted from near the touchline in the second half.

Warrington lost the Championship final 13-11 to Salford at Central Park but, five months later, returned to the same venue to defeat Barrow 8-4 in the Lancashire Cup final, with Brown crossing for Warrington's two tries. Brown played in all 42 of Warrington's games that season, scoring 20 tries as the Wire claimed the Lancashire League title for the first time in the club's history.

Brown started the 1938/39 season in similar form with four tries and eight goals (28 points) as Warrington won 37-4 at Rochdale. By the end of the campaign, however, war clouds were gathering over Europe and Brown returned home to Australia. He retired from playing at the age of twenty-eight, but continued to serve the game as a coach and administrator.

Brian Case
Prop-forward, 1976-82

Season	Apps	Tries	Pts
1975/76	1(1)	0	0
1976/77	17(4)	2	6
1977/78	23(10)	2	6
1978/79	37	3	9
1979/80	38	1	3
1980/81	37(1)	4	12
1981/82	21	2	8
TOTAL	**174(17)**	**14**	**42**

Brian Case was a solid, if unspectacular, prop who was deceptively strong and mobile. He was also yet another Warrington forward who learned his trade at Wilderspool before achieving even greater success elsewhere.

In his eight years with the Wire, Case collected just two winners' medals – for the Lancashire Cup triumph of 1980 and the John Player Trophy victory of 1981. His six years with Wigan brought him success on a much grander scale – in the World Club Challenge, Challenge Cup, Championship, Premiership, John Player Special Trophy and Lancashire Cup. He also toured Australia and New Zealand in 1984 and won 7 Great Britain caps. The Warrington coaching staff had taught him well.

St Helens-born Case joined Warrington, aged seventeen, from the Blackbrook amateur club in February 1975, receiving a £300 signing-on fee. Under the guidance of coach Alex Murphy and his assistant, Tommy Grainey, he quickly worked his way up through the Wire Colts and A teams before making his full debut in a surprise 17-13 victory at Hull Kingston Rovers in February 1976.

By the time he was twenty, Case was a first-team regular. He was also named Warrington's young player of the year in 1978/79 after a season in which he won the first of 4 Great Britain Under-24 caps, against France in Limoux.

Case – all 5ft 11in and 14st 7lb of him – was Warrington's most consistent forward in 1979/80, the club's centenary season, and he was rewarded with an England cap, again against France, at Headingley in February 1981.

With Case to the fore, Warrington swept all before them at start of the 1980/81 season, but missed out on the Championship and lost in the semi-finals of the Challenge Cup. After that, it was almost inevitable that Case would move on.

He made his last appearance at St Helens in March 1982, before a dispute with the club kept him out of the game for ten months. Case eventually joined Wigan for a fee approaching £45,000 in January 1983.

Case later spent two seasons with Leigh at the end of his playing career and was on the coaching staff at St Helens.

Jim Challinor
Centre, 1952-63

Season	Apps	Tries	Pts
1952/53	2	1	3
1953/54	36	19	57
1954/55	33	19	57
1955/56	8	2	6
1956/57	37	12	36
1957/58	24	15	45
1958/59	28	10	30
1959/60	35	14	42
1960/61	37	26	78
1961/62	16	7	21
1962/63	26	10	30
TOTAL	**282**	**135**	**405**

Challinor also kicked 2 drop goals.

Jim Challinor was the 'baby' of the brilliant Warrington team who succeeded in winning the Challenge Cup and Championship final double in the 1953/54 season and he matured to become one of the finest centres to feature in the club's history.

Furthermore, once his playing days were over, he became one of the game's top coaches. In 1972 alone, he guided St Helens to their Challenge Cup win over Leeds and Great Britain to their World Cup triumph in France.

He remained Great Britain coach for the 1974 tour of Australia and New Zealand and even played one game during the trip, because of an injury crisis, and scored a try. Tragically, two years later, in December 1976, he died of cancer at the age of just forty-two.

'When Jim was playing there were a lot of good centres around,' said Brian Bevan, 'but he was right at the top all the time. He was an unselfish player, a great centre – one of the best Warrington have had.' Bevan was talking from experience, because he and Challinor had been partners on Warrington's right flank almost 200 times. Included in that total were three Championship finals (1954, 1955 and 1961), the drawn 1954 Challenge Cup final and replay victory and the 1959 Lancashire Cup final win.

Challinor had joined Warrington from the Orford junior club in October 1952 and made his Wire debut as a raw teenager at home to St Helens the following month. Bevan was injured and Challinor, a strongly-built six-footer, played on the right wing.

Another key moment in his career arrived in January 1954, when Warrington signed Stan McCormick from St Helens and coach Cec Mountford decided to try Challinor as centre to Bevan. It was a great success and Mountford's first choice three-quarter line – Bevan, Challinor, Naughton, McCormick – is rated as one of the best the club have fielded.

Two and a half months later, Warrington had completed the 'double' and 'Chall', who was still only nineteen, had scored his nineteenth try of the season in the Challenge Cup final replay at Odsal in front of 102,569 supporters.

Bill Chapman
Loose-forward, 1935-47

Season	Apps	Tries	Pts
1935/36	28	2	6
1936/37	18	2	6
1937/38	40	8	24
1938/39	39	8	24
1939/40	26	4	12
1940/41	9	1	3
1945/46	4	1	3
1946/47	15	1	3
TOTAL	**179**	**27**	**81**

Bill Chapman was a Welsh loose-forward whose career was cut in half by the Second World War. Yet it was during that conflict that he achieved his greatest claim to fame. As Private W.G. Chapman, he played in the first Rugby League versus Rugby Union game, which took place on Saturday 23 January 1943, when he lined up for the Northern Command League XV against the Northern Command Union XV at Headingley.

Even though the game was played under union rules, the league boys still won 18-11 in front of 8,000 spectators. The experiment was repeated fifteen months later at Odsal Stadium on 29 April 1944, as a Combined Services Rugby Match to raise funds for services charities.

Newly-promoted Sergeant W.G. Chapman (Army, Warrington, Wales) again lined up as a back-row forward for the Rugby League against the Rugby Union and played his part in a 15-10 victory. That was to be the last cross-code clash until Wigan played Bath in May 1996 after rugby union, too, had become professional.

Legend has it that Chapman joined Warrington from Bridgend in 1935 after a chance meeting with former Wire scrum-half Dai Davies in a Blackpool pub. Chapman was on holiday with some friends and Davies, recognising a familiar accent, introduced himself. Chapman explained that he was running out of money and Davies offered to give him an advance if he agreed to play a trial match for Warrington's A team at Wilderspool. Chapman accepted the offer, impressed in the trial match and signed for Warrington.

Chapman made his first-team debut at Wilderspool in August 1935, but was controversially left out of Warrington's Challenge Cup final team against Leeds at Wembley the following April. He was, however, a key member of the team who won the Lancashire Cup by beating Barrow 8-4 in the final at Wigan in October 1937.

Chapman was also a member of the Wire side who finished second in the Northern Rugby League table in the 1936/37 season and reached the Championship final against league leaders Salford, only to lose 13-11.

Chapman played his last game for Warrington at Wilderspool in January 1947, having won 2 caps for the Welsh rugby league team in 1943 and 1944.

Dave Chisnall
Prop-forward, 1971-75 and 1981-84

Season	Apps	Tries	Pts
1971/72	10	1	3
1972/73	42	10	30
1973/74	39(3)	2	6
1974/75	42	11	33
1975/76	4	0	0
1981/82	24(1)	2	6
1982/83	22(8)	3	9
1983/84	11(4)	0	0
TOTAL	**194(16)**	**29**	**87**

Dave Chisnall was one of Warrington's greatest entertainers, being a prop-forward with a sense of humour and a flair for the dramatic. During his first spell with the club, 'Chissie' was one of the best props in the business, winning 4 England caps and making 5 appearances for Lancashire.

The front row of Chisnall, hooker Kevin Ashcroft and blindside-prop Brian Brady was the foundation for much of the remarkable success achieved by Alex Murphy's team.

Billy Benyon brought Chisnall back to Wilderspool in October 1981 for his strength, experience and bare-faced cheek. Against Bradford Northern at Wilderspool in September 1982, for example, Chisnall scored an outrageous try when he twice sold dummies to would-be tacklers on the half-way line before charging clear to touch down at the Railway End.

Chisnall had first signed for Warrington more than a decade earlier, in August 1971, when Murphy paid Leigh a club record £8,000 for the 5ft 9in, sixteen stone forward.

The following month he was sent off for flattening Peter Walker, the Bradford hooker, and banned for six matches, but he soon settled down to become one of the leading lights in the team. For three seasons, Chisnall hardly missed a match as Warrington won the League Leaders' rose bowl (1972/73), the Captain Morgan Trophy, the Player's No.6 Trophy, the Challenge Cup and the Club Championship (all 1973/74) and reached the BBC2 Floodlit Trophy final and Challenge Cup final again (both in 1974/75).

Chisnall was the Warrington captain for the return trip to Wembley but, five months later, he fell out with Murphy and was sold to Swinton for £5,000. Spells with Leigh, St Helens and Barrow followed before he returned to Wilderspool.

'It was an incredible honour for me to captain the side at Wembley,' said Chisnall. 'It was such a huge occasion. I was quite calm after we'd won it the year before but it was terribly disappointing when we lost. Playing at Wilderspool was always special, particularly in the big games. We had a big rivalry with Featherstone and Dewsbury during my first spell with the club and the ground was always packed when they came to play.

'I enjoyed coming back to play at the ground when I was at other clubs too. The fans always treated me as one of their own and there was a great rapport.'

Dave Cotton snr
Hooker, 1935-48

Season	Apps	Tries	Pts
1935/36	33	0	0
1936/37	44	2	6
1937/38	40	1	3
1938/39	39	0	0
1939/40	24	0	0
1940/41	16	1	3
1945/46	36	4	12
1946/47	43	0	0
1947/48	35	1	3
1948/49	16	0	0
TOTAL	**326**	**9**	**27**

Dave Cotton finished his Warrington career as the oldest player ever to represent the club; he was 39 years and 229 days old at his last appearance. He was also one of the best hookers in the business in an era when scrums were frequent and winning a plentiful supply of possession was essential.

Cotton joined Warrington from St Helens in November 1935, on the recommendation of Jack Arkwright, and he proved to be a master of his craft. In the 1936 Challenge Cup final against Leeds at Wembley, for example, Cotton saved Warrington from a thrashing by heeling the ball from 70 per cent of the scrums – but the Wire still lost 18-2.

The following year he scored a try, one of only nine touchdowns for the club, in the narrow Championship final defeat against Salford and collected a Lancashire Cup winners' medal against Barrow.

During the war, Dave Cotton often played for Huddersfield and Keighley as a 'guest' and appeared in the Yorkshire Cup finals of 1942 and 1943. Food was rationed at the time, but Cotton's match fee often included pieces of fish!

The highlight of his Wire career, however, came at the end of the epic 1947/48 season, when he was a vital member of the first Warrington side to win the championship. Cotton won the scrums 36-28 as Warrington beat Bradford Northern 15-5 in front of 69,341 supporters at Maine Road.

Six months later, Cotton retired, his last appearance coming in the 1948 Lancashire Cup final defeat against Wigan at Swinton in front of 39,015 fans. He did, however, perform one more outstanding service to the club when he recommended that they sign Ike Fishwick from St Helens as his replacement.

That, of course, is not the end of the Cotton story because his youngest son, Dave junior, followed him into the Warrington front row between 1967 and 1970. His oldest son, Fran, became a rugby union legend with England and the British Lions and a successful businessman.

Cotton was justifiably proud of both of them and accompanied them to watch a match at Wilderspool in 1989 as part of his eightieth birthday celebrations. He died, aged ninety, in December 1999.

Neil Courtney
Prop-forward, 1979-83

Season	Apps	Tries	Pts
1979/80	27	1	3
1980/81	36	0	0
1981/82	30(2)	2	6
1982/83	36	1	3
1983/84	2	0	0
TOTAL	**131(2)**	**4**	**12**

Neil Courtney was an old-fashioned, man-mountain of a prop who was Warrington's player of the season in the successive campaigns of 1980/81 and 1981/82 – no mean feat for a forward.

Weighing in at fifteen and a half stones and standing at 6ft 1in tall, Courtney was signed from St Helens in September 1979 and soon became the cornerstone of the Wire pack.

'I have never seen him have a bad game,' wrote John Bevan in his testimonial brochure, 'the odd super game, many good games and the odd average game. A real grafter. Anyone running into Neil needs a rest for five minutes.'

In the magnificent 1980/81 season, Courtney collected winners' medals in the Lancashire Cup and the John Player Trophy as Warrington swept all before them until fading towards the end of the season.

Courtney pocketed another Lancashire Cup winners' medal in October 1982 and his outstanding form was recognised when he won his only Great Britain cap as a substitute against Australia at Headingley in the third Test the following month.

Warrington team-mate Paul Cullen recalled: 'He was a massive man, really thickset, and a tough, uncompromising forward who never took a backwards step. He commanded respect from his opponents and from his team-mates alike. Off the pitch, he was very quiet. He or his father used to run a small pub in Lymm and occasionally we would have the odd team social there. He was a gentleman.'

Courtney joined Wigan in January 1984, where he fulfilled a lifelong ambition by receiving a Challenge Cup winners' medal against Hull in the classic 1985 final. Half the Wigan pack that glorious May afternoon (Courtney, Brian Case and Ian Potter) were former Warrington forwards.

Sadly, in February 1986, Courtney was forced to retire following a freak shoulder injury after just 43 full appearances for the Central Park club plus 4 more as a substitute.

Courtney's three years at St Helens at the start of his professional career had seen him make 45 appearances, including 9 as a substitute, before Warrington coach Billy Benyon, who had played alongside him at Knowsley Road, took him to Wilderspool. It was an inspired move.

Paul Cullen
Stand-off, centre and back-row forward, 1981-96

Season	Apps	Tries	Pts
1981/82	15(1)	1	3
1982/83	38(1)	6	18
1983/84	8	1	4
1984/85	11	3	12
1985/86	32(1)	4	16
1986/87	21)	9	36
1987/88	27(1)	7	28
1988/89	15(3)	2	8
1989/90	8(3)	3	12
1990/91	28(2)	2	8
1991/92	12(8)	0	0
1992/93	30	6	24
1993/94	19	2	8
1994/95	26	5	20
1995/96	19	2	8
1996	21	3	12
TOTAL	**330(20)**	**56**	**217**

Warrington's defence has not been as fearsome or as feared since Paul Cullen was forced to retire with a persistent knee injury.

When Cullen was in his prime even top-class internationals like David Topliss, the Wakefield Trinity and Hull half-back, breathed a sigh of relief when he was absent through injury or suspension.

With Cullen in the team, Warrington could go to Wigan and win 6-4, as they did on New Year's Day 1987, with Cullen scoring the only try of the match. Cullen was not the only Warrington player who could tackle, but he certainly did more than his fair share.

That is why six different Warrington coaches – Billy Benyon, Kevin Ashcroft, Reg Bowden, Tony Barrow, Brian Johnson and John Dorahy – made Cullen the first name on the team-sheet. A sound defence wins matches.

Cullen's playing career spanned fifteen years and four different positions – stand-off (51 appearances), centre (125), loose-forward (55) and second-row forward (99). He also served the club as commercial manager and, later, as assistant coach to Darryl Van de Velde. Cullen was also caretaker coach for one match following John Dorahy's sudden departure in March 1997 and he guided Warrington to a remarkable 35-24 victory over Wigan at a sun-drenched Wilderspool.

He signed for Warrington from Crosfields in November 1980 and made his debut in a Lancashire Cup tie at Barrow the following August. His first try also came against Barrow, at Wilderspool in April 1982, and was voted Warrington's try of the season.

That summer, Cullen and centre Ronnie Duane went on the first Great Britain Colts tour, to Papua New Guinea and Australia, and played in the feature matches against the Young Kumuls and the Young Kangaroos.

On their return to England, the pair quickly collected Lancashire Cup winners' medals as Warrington thrashed St Helens 16-0 in the final at Central Park. Cullen's Wire career had got off to a dream start, but Warrington's substitute forward that day,

Young gun: Stand-off Paul Cullen makes a break against Barrow at Wilderspool during his first season in the first-team with John Bevan in support (left).

the veteran Dave Chisnall, told him to make the most of it because dark days certainly lay ahead.

How right he was. The biggest disappointment came in the spring of 1990 when Cullen was banned for eight matches for a high tackle, a suspension that ruled him out of Warrington's Wembley line-up against Wigan. Cullen's first game as captain, at St Helens in January 1996, was also another low point as Warrington suffered a humiliating 80-0 defeat in a Regal Trophy semi-final.

Fortunately, there were many more good days than bad, notably the Premiership Trophy success over Halifax in May 1986 and the Regal Trophy win over Bradford Northern in January 1991. Cullen also made 3 appearances for Lancashire.

'I signed for £2,000 so I think they have got their money's worth,' said Cullen in an interview in 1999. 'I got into the first team in 1981 – that was the Ken Kelly, Tommy Martyn, Steve Hesford, Bob Eccles team – when the win bonus was £500 but there was no contract money, so it was a completely different philosophy.

'If you didn't win, you didn't eat. That's where the drive and hunger came from. These days guys are on executive salaries win, lose or draw. It is a completely different world and a completely different philosophy to coach these players as well. I wish I was playing today.' And so say all of us.

Billy Cunliffe
Prop-forward, 1914-30

Season	Apps	Tries	Pts
1914/15	29	2	6
1918/19	16	0	0
1919/20	29	5	15
1920/21	28	3	9
1921/22	31	3	9
1922/23	35	3	9
1923/24	36	9	27
1924/25	33	5	15
1925/26	40	5	15
1926/27	38	0	0
1927/28	39	0	0
1928/29	40	3	9
1929/30	42	0	0
1930/31	2	0	0
TOTAL	**438**	**38**	**114**

Billy Cunliffe also kicked 6 goals.

Billy and Tommy Cunliffe are the only brothers to appear in this volume and nobody could argue with their inclusion. Between them they made more than 750 appearances for the Wire and they were the backbone of the Warrington pack for more than a decade.

With Billy at number 8 and Tom at number 11, Warrington won the Lancashire Cup for the first time by beating Oldham 7-5 in front of 18,000 fans at the Cliff (which later became Manchester United's training ground) in December 1921. Again with Billy at No. 8 and Tommy at No. 11, Warrington reached the Championship final for the first time in 1926 – only to lose 22-10 to Wigan in front of 20,000 fans at Knowsley Road.

The Cunliffes joined Warrington within a couple of months of each other in 1914 from the Pemberton Rovers amateur club. Billy, the elder, made his debut at home to Barrow in the Lancashire Cup that October and Tommy followed him into the Warrington pack at Batley two months later.

Their careers were soon interrupted by the First World War, but when hostilities had ceased the pair continued where they had left off. Billy played almost all of his career as a prop-forward while Tommy was at home almost anywhere in the pack.

They were also a couple of characters and the late Jackie Hamblett, who worked on the Warrington groundstaff for sixty years, loved to tell the story of how they tried to outdo each other by being first in the bath after a game to get the benefit of the hottest and cleanest water. On one occasion, they both jumped into the bath together only to discover the water was too hot. They both let out a yell and jumped out again, but Tommy, determined not to be beaten, ran back into the dressing room, puts his socks back on and returned to the bath undaunted.

When Hamblett first arrived at Wilderspool in 1920, as a lad of sixteen, he used to make himself useful by doing all sorts of jobs, such as helping with the kit. The players soon realised he was not being paid and Billy and Tommy Cunliffe, together with Jim Tranter, formed a deputation on his behalf to insist that the directors put the matter right. They

Tommy Cunliffe
Forward, 1914-28

Season	Apps	Tries	Pts
1914/15	21	3	9
1918/19	13	1	3
1919/20	26	5	15
1920/21	37	8	24
1921/22	38	4	12
1922/23	38	10	30
1923/24	32	1	3
1924/25	25	4	12
1925/26	40	5	15
1926/27	25	3	9
1927/28	26	4	12
1928/29	3	0	0
TOTAL	**324**	**48**	**144**

emerged from the boardroom to announce to Jackie that he was now on the staff and was to be paid four shillings and sixpence for first-team duties and three shillings for A team duties.

Tommy scored more tries than Billy for Warrington (48 against 38) but Billy was clearly the better player and his talents were frequently recognised by the selectors. He won 11 Great Britain caps, 10 England caps and made 19 appearances for Lancashire. He was also the first Warrington player to be chosen for two tours of Australia and New Zealand, in 1920 and 1924.

Billy, who was 5ft 10in and 14st 10lb, was the type of forward who could play his game to suit the occasion and his opponents soon learned to appreciate this. He could be skilful or he could be rough, tough and ruthless.

On the 1920 tour, Australia won the first two Tests but for the last one Billy and his Warrington team-mate Arthur Skelhorne were brought into the two prop positions for their Tests debuts. Both were instrumental in stopping the Kangaroos from securing a clean sweep as the Lions won 23-13 at the Royal Agricultural Ground, Sydney.

When the Kangaroos came to England in 1921/22, Cunliffe and Skelhorne were the cornerstones of the pack as Great Britain won the series 2-1. On his second tour, Cunliffe was still the first-choice No. 8 for the three Tests as the Ashes were retained.

The Cunliffes were awarded a joint testimonial season in 1927/28 and each received the princely sum of £187/17/8. Tommy made his 324th and final appearance in primrose and blue at the now defunct Wigan Highfield club in November 1928.

Billy's career, however, was far from over and he was a member of the Warrington team who reached the 1928 Challenge Cup final against Swinton at Wigan, only to lose 5-3 after they were reduced to twelve men by injury. He also collected a second Lancashire Cup winners' medal in November 1929, when Warrington beat Salford 15-2 in front of 21,012 fans in the final at Wigan.

Billy made his 438th and final appearance for the Wire against Wigan at Wilderspool in September 1930, almost sixteen years after he had made his debut.

Dai Davies
Scrum-half, 1927-34

Season	Apps	Tries	Pts
1927/28	20	3	9
1928/29	4	0	0
1929/30	33	4	12
1930/31	17	0	0
1931/32	39	9	27
1932/33	37	10	30
1933/34	36	7	21
1934/35	10	1	3
TOTAL	**196**	**34**	**102**

You could write a book about the life and times of Warrington's Welsh scrum-half Dai Morgan Davies. Indeed, somebody has, and Man of Amman – The Life of Dai Davies, written by Phil Melling and published in March 1994, is a fascinating account of a bygone age. In it we learn how proud Davies was to play for Warrington, to the extent that he still wore his club blazer long after he had retired to South Wales. We also learn about his run-ins with authority and gain a vivid impression of what a confident player he was in his pomp.

Davies should have toured Australia and New Zealand with Great Britain in 1932, but missed out because of his sometimes abrasive personality. He did, however, achieve an unwelcome sort of fame by becoming the first player to play on the loing side in four Challenge Cup finals. Two of those finals were with Warrington, in 1928 and 1933, and they were followed by one each with Huddersfield (1935) and Keighley (1937), when Davies was the unlucky captain.

Davies joined Warrington from the now defunct Broughton Rangers club in November 1927 for £650 – a massive fee at the time – and his half-back partnership with fellow Welshman Tommy Flynn developed into one of the best in the club's history.

Davies started the 1928 Challenge Cup final on the wing, but reverted to scrum-half following an injury to Billy Kirk. He was, however, powerless to prevent Swinton winning 5-3. The 1933 final was probably his finest hour in a Warrington shirt, with Davies capping a brilliant display with two tries in a heart-breaking 21-17 defeat.

There have not been many scrum-halves who have been quicker from the base of a scrum and his blind-side break was lightning quick and devastating to all opposition. His sleight of hand was hypnotic.

'I never regretted signing for Warrington,' said Davies. 'They treated me well. There was no soccer team, only rugby in Warrington, and the Rugby Union team was nil. They all came to watch us – we were the idols of the town.'

When his playing days were over, he returned to Wilderspool as a trainer and scout, giving many more years of devoted service. He died in Ammanford, aged eighty-nine, in February 1992.

Jonathan Davies
Centre, 1993-95

Season	Apps	Tries	Goals	Pts
1993/94	30	21	99	293
1994/95	29	18	104	292
1995/96	7	4	29	77
TOTAL	**66**	**43**	**232**	**662**

Davies also kicked 26 drop goals.

One man does not make a team – but one man can make a huge difference, as Jonathan Davies proved during his two years at Wilderspool.

The season before Davies arrived, Warrington finished eighth in the Stones Bitter Championship, with more defeats than victories. They needed a top-quality goalkicker, pace in the centres and a proven match-winner. Davies was all three rolled into one.

During his first season with the Wire, he was the club's leading try-scorer and goalkicker as Warrington pushed Wigan and Bradford Northern all the way to the title. He was also named Man of Steel (Man of the Season) and voted the First Division Player of the Year by his fellow professionals.

Davies had been signed on a free transfer from Widnes, aged thirty, in July 1993. The Chemics were in dire financial straits and could no longer afford his £75,000-a-season contract. Warrington stepped in with sponsorship being provided by chairman Peter Higham's employers Hertel UK Ltd. It was money well spent.

Among the many golden memories of his Warrington career, two matches stand out – at Halifax in the fourth round of the Challenge Cup in January 1994 and at Keighley in the quarter-finals of the Regal Trophy the following year. On both occasions Warrington were losing (12-4 at Halifax and 18-8 at Keighley) before Davies turned the tables with spectacular tries and coolly-taken goals.

Davies won 4 Great Britain caps and 7 Wales caps during his time at Wilderspool. He also scored one of the great Great Britain tries when, from the full-back position, his pace created an opening out of nothing and paved the way for an 8-4 victory over Australia at Wembley in October 1994.

He was also awarded the MBE for services to both codes of rugby. Not surprisingly, when rugby union became professional, Davies was the first player the fifteen-a-side code wanted back. He joined Cardiff in October 1995 in a reported £100,000 deal and went on to play for Wales again. These days he is a highly-respected pundit on both codes of rugby for the BBC.

'League is a wonderful game, and above all honest,' said Jonathan Davies in an interview earlier this year. 'You work like hell and get your head kicked in at times, but the people in it are totally genuine.'

George Dickenson
Centre, 1900-14

Season	Apps	Tries	Pts
1900/01	21	7	21
1901/02	32	6	18
1902/03	26	5	15
1903/04	34	9	27
1904/05	26	4	12
1905/06	16	1	3
1906/07	25	13	39
1907/08	35	15	45
1908/09	32	12	36
1909/10	31	10	30
1910/11	32	6	18
1911/12	29	5	15
1912/13	11	0	0
1913/14	25	1	3
TOTAL	**375**	**94**	**282**

Dickenson also kicked 14 goals.

George Dickenson was at the heart of one of Warrington's greatest three-quarter lines. For something like five seasons and 170 matches, the quartet of Jack Fish, Danny Isherwood, George Dickenson and Elliott Harris were idolised by Warrington supporters and feared by the rest of the League. Even the most hardened sportswriters of the day called them 'poetry in motion'.

Dickenson, who was 5ft 10in tall and weighed 11 stones 6lb, was a top-class centre and set up dozens of tries for whichever winger he was partnering. He played in four Challenge Cup finals, collecting losers' medals in 1901 and 1904 against Batley and Halifax respectively and enjoying the triumphs of 1905 and 1907 against Hull Kingston Rovers and Oldham.

He made his mark in representative matches, too, winning 4 England caps and making 4 appearances for Lancashire. He also won a Great Britain cap when he lined up in the first Test match against Australia at Park Royal, London on 12 December 1908. The match ended in a 22-22 draw.

Dickenson was named Warrington captain for the 1909/10 season and made his final appearance for the club on 18 March 1914 at Runcorn. According to the accounts for 1903/04, Dickenson received £4 to sign on for that season, with match fees of 17s 6d for a win and 12s 6d for a draw or a defeat. He was worth every penny.

It is interesting to note that, in one way, Dickenson was the odd man out in Warrington's magnificent three-quarter line of 1900 to 1906. If, for example, his surname had been Simpson then the initials of the four would have spelt out FISH. Incidentally, there were two occasions in 1900 when that was the case. First, in January, when Fish, Isherwood, Smith and Harris played and, the following month, when the line-up was Fish, Isherwood, Smith and Hockenhall.

Billy Dingsdale
Centre, 1928-40

Season	Apps	Tries	Pts
1928/29	33	28	84
1929/30	34	25	75
1930/31	38	16	48
1931/32	36	12	36
1932/33	35	25	75
1933/34	30	9	27
1934/35	39	7	21
1935/36	21	8	24
1936/37	24	8	24
1937/38	28	6	18
1938/39	36	7	21
1939/40	19	3	9
TOTAL	**373**	**154**	**462**

Dingsdale also kicked 4 goals.

Billy Dingsdale was Warrington's classiest centre and deserved many more than his 3 Great Britain caps. He signed for Warrington from Broughton Rangers in September 1928 for £600 – at a time when the world record fee was only £1,000. Dingsdale himself was also given a £100 signing-on fee.

At 5ft 11in and 12st 4lb, he was a great stylist and Warrington have probably never had a more creative centre and, from a try-scoring perspective, only Ally Naughton has scored more from the centre positions.

Dingsdale was an expert at creating openings for his winger and his partnership with Tommy 'Tubby' Thompson was very productive. 'Tubby' was not blessed with speed, but if he were given the ball 20 yards out with just one man to beat a try could be guaranteed because he had a wonderful sidestep.

Dingsdale had the ability to do just that and he was an expert at a skill not seen today – approaching an opponent at top speed, chipping the ball over his head with the outside of his boot, accelerating round the player and catching the ball before it landed.

The first of 7 England caps arrived in the 1928/29 season and he made his Great Britain debut against Australia at Hull the following year. He also played 14 times for Lancashire.

But what should have been the highlight of his career, going on the 1932 Great Britain tour of Australia and New Zealand, turned out to be a big disappointment because he could only play a handful of games due to injury.

He was also unlucky to play for Warrington at a time when they were the nearly men of rugby league, losing the Challenge Cup finals of 1933 and 1936 and the Championship finals of 1935 and 1937. At least Dingsdale had the honour of being the first Warrington player to score a try at Wembley, against Huddersfield in 1933, and he collected Lancashire Cup winners' medals in 1929 and 1932.

Dingsdale's brothers, Tommy and Ben, were also fine rugby league players. Tommy gave great service to St Helens Recs, York, Lancashire and England while Ben made 9 appearances for Warrington in 1928.

When he retired from playing, Dingsdale became licensee of the Stanley Arms pub in St Helens for twenty-five years. He died in hospital in St Helens on 14 September 1965, aged sixty.

Des Drummond
Winger, 1987-92

Season	Apps	Tries	Pts
1986/87	17	8	32
1987/88	31	18	72
1988/89	31	12	48
1989/90	37	14	56
1990/91	37	9	36
1991/92	29	8	32
TOTAL	**182**	**69**	**276**

Des Drummond was the last Warrington captain to lift a trophy, but he is best remembered for his 'specials' – length-of-the-field tries where he would slice through the opposition to the delight of supporters.

Drummond scored Warrington's try of the season in 1987/88 (against St Helens at Wilderspool) and in 1988/89 (at Hull Kingston Rovers) with just such efforts. Writer and broadcaster Ray French was one of his many admirers. 'He was a most difficult opponent to stop,' said French, 'bouncing from tacklers like a rubber ball and bursting forth with tremendous acceleration when in the clear. Nor was he shy in the tackle, using all the expertise of his black belt judo training to topple and thwart the biggest of opponents.'

Drummond was born in Jamaica in June 1958 and spent ten years with Leigh – scoring 141 tries in 280 appearances – before joining Warrington for £40,000 in February 1987. He scored on his debut, against Bradford Northern at Wilderspool, and never looked back, rarely missing a match through injury and always providing a threat on the right wing.

Drummond, 5ft 8in and 11st 3lb, was Warrington's leading try-scorer in 1987/88 and was a key member of the team who won the Lancashire Cup in 1989. Later that season, he fulfilled a lifelong ambition when he played at Wembley against Wigan in the Challenge Cup final.

When Mike Gregory, Warrington's Wembley captain, was injured, Drummond was the obvious choice to take over the reins and so it fell to him to collect the Regal Trophy after the 12-2 victory over Bradford at Headingley in January 1991.

Drummond also won 2 Great Britain caps while at Wilderspool and would have gone on the 1988 tour of Australia and New Zealand but for an unsavoury incident at Widnes, eight days before the squad departed, when he was confronted by a spectator on the pitch.

Drummond hit the fan, but was later cleared of an assault charge and was found to have acted in self defence. The verdict, of course, came long after the tour had finished.

From then on, Drummond refused to give interviews but continued to do his talking on the pitch and was the Supporters' Club Player of the Year in 1989/90. Drummond finished his career at Workington, adding 32 more tries to an already impressive tally.

Ronnie Duane
Centre, 1981-89

Season	Apps	Tries	Pts
1981/82	14(3)	3	9
1982/83	36	11	33
1983/84	36	16	64
1984/85	5(1)	2	8
1985/86	14(1)	6	24
1986/87	24(3)	7	28
1987/88	13(1)	3	12
1988/89	14(2)	2	8
1989/90	2(4)	1	4
TOTAL	**158(15)**	**51**	**190**

Duane also kicked 28 goals.

Oh, what might have been. Warrington supporters who witnessed the emergence of centre Ronnie Duane in the early 1980s were convinced they were watching an international star in the making and such was the power of his running that tabloid journalists even gave him the nickname 'Rhino'.

Agonisingly, it all went wrong during the opening match of the Great Britain tour to Australia and New Zealand in the summer of 1984. Duane lasted only eight minutes against Northern Territory in Darwin before he tore knee ligaments on the hard ground and was forced to return home. Duane, who was twenty-one two weeks after the fateful match, spent his birthday party in a wheelchair with his injured leg in plaster.

Of course, Duane battled his way back to fitness, but he never quite recaptured the pace and power that had seen him earn 3 Great Britain caps against France and score 16 tries in 36 appearances for Warrington during the 1983/84 season.

Duane was born in Warrington in May 1963 and learned the game with Woolston Rovers before signing for the Wire in April 1981, following in the footsteps of his brother Ian. Ronnie made his Warrington debut, aged eighteen, at Hull that October and was selected – with team-mate Paul Cullen – for the first Great Britain Colts tour of Papua New Guinea and Australia in June 1982.

Duane, who was 6ft 1in and 13st 10lb, was being groomed for the national side and, to that end, also made 2 appearances for the Great Britain Under-24s in 1983, scoring a try in each match. He also collected his first winners' medal, against St Helens in the 1982 Lancashire Cup final.

Further winners' medals followed in the second half of his playing career, in the 1986 Premiership final against Halifax and as a substitute forward in the 1989 Lancashire Cup final against Oldham. The following August, he was transferred to Oldham and he later played for Rochdale at the end of a career that had begun with such tantalising promise.

Bob Eccles
Prop or second-row forward, 1977-87

Season	Apps	Tries	Pts
1977/78	23(8)	6	18
1978/79	17(15)	5	15
1979/80	27(7)	4	12
1980/81	32(9)	15	45
1981/82	21(4)	8	24
1982/83	37	37	111
1983/84	34(1)	19	76
1984/85	33	18	72
1985/86	11	6	24
1986/87	4(8)	1	4
TOTAL	**239(52)**	**119**	**401**

Eccles also kicked 30 goals and 8 drop goals.

Almost fifteen years after his final appearance for Warrington, Bob Eccles remains the highest try-scoring forward in the club's history and his record looks safe for a good while yet. Eccles was also a great entertainer and scorer of spectacular tries, qualities which were recognised by Andy Gregory, who named Eccles in his Fantasy Rugby League XIII in his biography *Pint Size: Heroes and Hangovers*.

'Bob's selection might come as a bit of a surprise to some people, but I really rated this fellow,' wrote Gregory. 'His record of tries for a back-row forward speaks for itself. He had bags of pace, and although he came into the game late, he made up for lost time by fulfilling his ambition of playing for Great Britain.

'Obviously, Bob needed someone to put him through the gap in the first place, but once he had the ball there was no stopping him. There are plenty of forwards these days who are looking for support after about five yards, but he always had the confidence in his own ability to make the line. And he usually did.'

Eccles was at his best in the 1982/83 season, when he scored a remarkable 37 tries in 37 appearances – including five in one match against Blackpool Borough – to become the leading scorer in the game. His form even earned him a place in the Great Britain side to face Australia in the Second Test at Wigan's Central Park that November. It was a baptism of fire. The Kangaroos had already won the first Test at Hull 40-4 and Great Britain coach Johnny Whiteley had made ten changes for the second instalment of the Ashes series. Australia were unchanged and romped to a 27-6 victory.

Eccles was never invited to wear the red, white and blue of Great Britain again, although he continued to torment defences in the primrose and blue of Warrington until a twice broken right arm virtually ended his career in the top division. He suffered the first break in the 1985 Lancashire Cup final defeat against Wigan and the second in his comeback game against St Helens the following January.

Eccles was born in St Helens in July 1957 and was discovered by the then Warrington coach Alex Murphy playing soccer for

Crash, bang, wallop: Bob Eccles leaves two Bradford Northern defenders trailing in his wake as he heads for the try line at Wilderspool on the opening day of the 1985/86 season.

Culcheth in a local league, although he had played rugby league for Rochdale Hornets Colts between November 1976 and March 1977.

Eccles, who was 6ft 1in and 15st 4lb, made his Wire debut against Salford at Wilderspool in September 1977 and really made a name for himself that November in the John Player Trophy semi-final at Wakefield. Eccles, still only twenty, scored a cracking solo try and helped to set one up for Ken Kelly as Warrington built up a match-winning 10-0 lead before half-time.

He collected John Player winners' medals in 1978 and 1981 and Lancashire Cup winners' medals in 1980 and 1982 as the try tally continued to rise. From September to November 1982, for example, he even scored in nine consecutive matches – another record for a Warrington forward.

Finally, at Bradford in April 1984, he broke Harry Bath's club record of 90 tries for a forward, but he was still far from finished. His 100th try arrived the following season and many more would undoubtedly have followed but for those broken arms.

'Bob Eccles is one of the fastest forwards I have ever seen,' wrote John Bevan in his testimonial brochure. 'When he sees the line, you need a crowbar to get the ball out of his hands. He has scored tries that a flying winger would have been proud to claim.'

Eccles was sold to Second Division Springfield Borough in August 1987 for £25,000 and later coached Blackpool Gladiators, Chorley and at Crosfields. Today, he remains a regular and popular visitor to Wilderspool.

47

Jackie Edwards
Scrum-half, 1955-64

Season	Apps	Tries	Pts
1955/56	2	0	0
1956/57	0	0	0
1957/58	38	8	28*
1958/59	38	13	39
1959/60	35	12	36
1960/61	39	14	42
1961/62	35	18	54
1962/63	26	11	33
1963/64	10	2	6
TOTAL	**223**	**78**	**238**

*Edwards also kicked 2 goals.

Jackie Edwards was one of Warrington's greatest scrum-halves, even though his career and his working life were cut horribly short by a spinal injury at the age of twenty-four. The playing career he should have had and the honours he should have won can be seen in the medals collection of his son, Shaun, the former Wigan and Great Britain scrum-half.

Both men were spotted as players of outstanding talent while still schoolboys in their hometown, Wigan. Jackie had been a prolific try-scorer in schools rugby and had become the youngest player to captain Lancashire County Schools, where he formed a lethal half-back combination with a young Alex Murphy.

Warrington's Cec Mountford was convinced Edwards would be a star of the future and signed him at Blackpool on his sixteenth birthday in August 1955. Warrington had completed the Championship and Challenge Cup double in 1953/54 and retained the Championship in 1954/55 but, disappointingly for coach and player, they were never to reach such dizzy heights again.

In fact, Jackie's only winners' medal during his nine seasons at Wilderspool came for the Lancashire Cup triumph against St Helens at Central Park, Wigan in October 1959. Warrington won 5-4 in front of almost 30,000 fans. Edwards was also the scrum-half in the 1961 Championship final at Odsal, when Warrington lost 25-10 to Leeds in front of a 52,000 crowd.

The closest he came to playing at Wembley – a ground which became his son's second home – was when Warrington lost 5-2 to Wakefield Trinity in the Challenge Cup semi-final at Swinton in April 1963. Edwards was also involved in the key incident in the game. Joe Pickavance, the Warrington centre, was in possession and running towards the Wakefield line with Edwards in support. Edwards is supposed to have called out 'Pick! Pick!' to let the centre know he was there for a pass as they neared Neil Fox, the Wakefield centre. Pickavance thought he had heard a shout of 'Kick! Kick!' and duly kicked the ball ahead. Fox collected with ease and a glorious try-scoring chance had disappeared. Wakefield went on to win the Cup by beating Wigan 25-10 in the final.

A few months later, Edwards' career was over. His final game was as a stand-off at Whitehaven in a Western Championship match in January 1964. Warrington lost 5-0. He was granted a testimonial year in 1966/67 which raised £750. While at Wilderspool, Edwards twice played for Lancashire in the County Championship.

Jim Featherstone
Prop or second-row forward, 1946-53

Season	Apps	Tries	Pts
1945/46	17	4	12
1946/47	41	5	15
1947/48	38	10	30
1948/49	36	11	33
1949/50	35	3	9
1950/51	25	1	3
1951/52	31	10	30
1952/53	17	3	9
TOTAL	**240**	**47**	**141**

Featherstone also kicked 2 goals and a drop goal.

Jim Featherstone was a Great Britain forward who enjoyed a huge appetite for food, fun and for rugby league. Bob Ryan, who played alongside him for club and country, was staggered by the amount his close friend could eat. Tommy Lomax, the Warrington physio, was flummoxed when Featherstone helped to make his bedroom vanish.

The disappearing trick happened in Cumbria in the days before the M6 was built and an important away game meant spending the night before in a guest house. On one occasion, after players and staff had put their bags in their rooms and headed downstairs for a meal, Featherstone and team-mate Harry Bath spotted a huge wardrobe on the landing, which was next to Lomax's bedroom door. Featherstone, 5ft 11in and 14st, and Bath, 6ft and 14st 7lb, effortlessly moved it along until the entrance was totally obscured and waited for the fun to start. Shortly after, Lomax retired to bed before returning with a puzzled look on his face. 'You won't believe this lads,' he said. 'I've lost my bedroom.'

Featherstone had played for his hometown club, Wigan, during the Second World War after joining them from the Ince Rangers amateur club. He moved to Warrington in late 1945 and was a stalwart of the pack for the next seven years before being transferred to Belle Vue Rangers in the deal that brought Welsh stand-off Ray Price to Wilderspool.

Those seven years brought him 6 Great Britain caps, 8 England caps and 6 appearances for Lancashire during rugby league's golden age when fans were flocking to see matches in unprecedented numbers. Featherstone earned two of those Great Britain caps against New Zealand during the 1950 tour, selection for which was something of a mixed blessing. It was the last tour party to travel by sea and so had to leave before the end of the season. For the good of the national team, Featherstone and Ryan had to miss the Challenge Cup final against Widnes at Wembley – which Warrington won 19-0 – and board the slow boat to Australia.

Ryan would play at Wembley in 1954, but Featherstone would never have another chance. The pair had already made history, however, by forming the second-row partnership in the first Warrington team to be crowned champions, at Maine Road in 1948. Both players were worthy champions.

Jack Fish
Right winger, 1898-1911

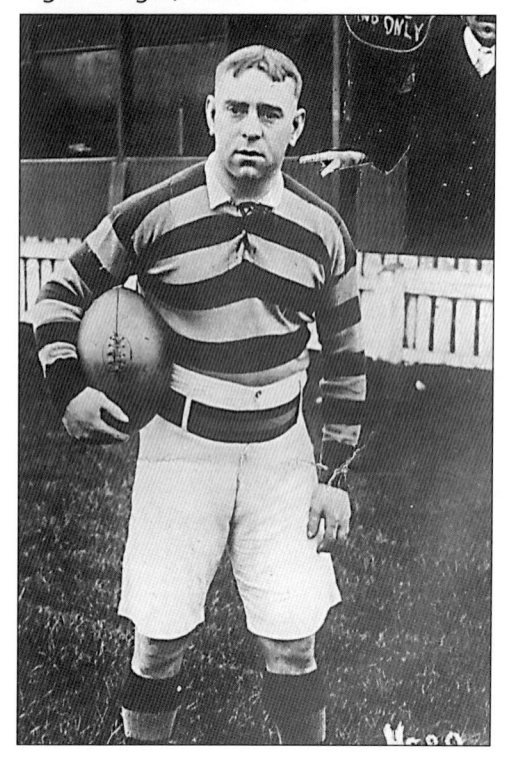

Season	Apps	Tries	Goals	Pts
1898/99	15	8	0	24
1899/00	21	16	14	76
1900/01	29	22	26	118
1901/02	28	16	23	94
1902/03	26	9	14	55
1903/04	36	16	29	106
1904/05	33	15	25	95
1905/06	16	7	15	51
1906/07	24	24	38	148
1907/08	26	25	13	101
1908/09	33	26	43	164
1909/10	29	28	22	128
1910/11	5	3	0	9
TOTAL	**321**	**215**	**262**	**1169**

Jack Fish was Warrington's first superstar and he remains the only player in the club's history to have scored 200 tries and kicked 200 goals. Only Brian Bevan has scored more tries for Warrington, but even Bevan could not equal Fish's record in the Challenge Cup.

Fish grabbed both tries in the 1905 final when the Wirepullers, as they were known, beat Hull Kingston Rovers 6-0 at Headingley to lift the trophy for the first time. Two years later, Fish was the captain as Oldham were thrashed 17-3 in the final at Broughton, with Fish scoring a try and kicking four goals. Fish also played in the losing sides in the 1901 and 1904 finals and later trained the Warrington team who reached the final in 1928. No wonder he was idolised by his own supporters and feared by his opponents.

Fish learned his rugby in a small village called Lostock Gralam, near Northwich, having moved there from Runcorn with his family as a small boy, and his sporting prowess soon became evident when he joined the village team. News filtered through to Wilderspool of his incredible speed and skills and a friendly was organised between the Warrington A team and a Lostock XV in October 1898. Suitably impressed, the Warrington committee arranged a meeting with young Jackie to discuss a signing-on fee.

The story goes that when he entered the committee room he was confronted by a table heaped high with £50 in silver, a rare sight in those days, and from then on the signing was a formality. He was selected for the next first-team match, a friendly against Barrow, and scored a sensational try. The following week at Rochdale, he made his full debut and went on to play 321 games for the club.

Fish was a stocky man, only 5ft 7in and 11st 8lb, but his speed off the mark was phenomenal and, blessed with a remarkable ability to take awkward passes, he was a formidable opponent. He could also stop dead in his tracks while at full speed, leaving would-be tacklers whizzing into touch, and such was his confidence and skill that, after crossing near the corner flag, he would often beat another couple of defenders to score under the posts.

In one game against Huddersfield in 1906, he scored 30 points from four tries and nine goals and it is on record that as he was placing the ball to kick for goal after scoring his fourth

Dedicated followers of fashion: Jack Fish (left) and the Australian centre Dan Frawley (who played 19 games for Warrington in the 1909/10 season, scoring 8 tries).

try the returning Huddersfield players and the referee congratulated him by patting him on the head.

Not surprisingly, Fish excelled at the sprint challenges that were common at the time. Wigan had a flier called Peter 'Bucky' Green and a match was arranged between the two at Springfield Park, Wigan, with a £100 side bet; Fish won at a canter.

In 1905, in a Challenge Cup tie against Warrington, Fred Cooper of Bradford, the AAA sprint champion of 1898, who had recorded 10 seconds for the 100 yards dash, tried in vain to catch Fish as he scorched away for a long-range try.

Fish was a legend in his own lifetime and played his final match for the Wire on 18 February 1911, at Coventry and, true to form, scored a try – the 215th of his Warrington career. He won all the possible honours of his day, playing twice for England, scoring three tries and kicking two goals. He also scored an amazing 16 tries and 12 goals during 16 appearances for Lancashire and he was only robbed of a place on the Great Britain tour to Australia in 1910 by injury. He was awarded a testimonial match in 1910 and received the sum of £268 15s 11d.

When war broke out in 1914, Fish enlisted in the army and, at the age of thirty-five, won the Aldershot Command Sprint Championship, but was invalided out with chest problems shortly afterwards.

Fish died on 23 October 1940, but the exploits that thrilled the fans in those early years will live long in the annals of Wilderspool. In his pomp, the fans even dedicated a verse to him:

Stuntz can run, and then he's done,
Catch a ball and that is all,
Geo Dicky is very tricky,
very light and tall.
Brookes looks fine
when he is bound for the line.
But I would rather see Fish on
when he is in condition
the lad can beat them all.

Jackie Fleming
Stand-off, 1947-49

Season	Apps	Tries	Pts
1946/47	18	8	24
1947/48	34	5	15
1948/49	35	6	18
1949/50	17	7	21
TOTAL	**104**	**26**	**78**

Jack Fleming, rather like Kevin Ashcroft, served Warrington with distinction as a player and, later, as a coach. Fleming formed a formidable half-back combination with Gerry Helme and was the stand-off in the first Warrington team to be crowned champions, when they defeated Bradford Northern 15-5 in the Championship final at Maine Road in May 1948.

He was appointed Warrington coach in May 1967, guiding the Wire to the Lancashire League title and Lancashire Cup final in the 1967/68 season. Like most coaches, however, he was sacked – at 10 p.m. on Wednesday 18 December 1968 after a 16-9 defeat at home to Leeds, although the decision had already been made before the match. Fleming was told he was not getting the best out of the players and that there was friction in the camp after he had disciplined some players for missing training.

Wigan-born Fleming joined his hometown club from Newtown Legion in 1940 and played on the wing in both legs of the Championship final as Wigan were crowned champions of the War Emergency League in May 1943. He was also the stand-off in the 1945 Lancashire Cup final, when Wigan were beaten 7-3 by Widnes in front of a crowd of 28,184 at Wilderspool.

Wigan's signing of New Zealander Cec Mountford spelt the end of his time at Central Park and he joined Warrington in January 1947 for £600. Keighley, Swinton and Belle Vue Rangers had also been trying to sign the twenty-five-year-old miner. Over the next three years, he played in three major finals and won 5 England caps as Warrington revelled in rugby league's golden age.

Fleming played in consecutive Championship finals (1948 and 1949) and in the 1948 Lancashire Cup final against Wigan at Station Road, Swinton. He also played in front of Wilderspool's record crowd – the 34,304 who turned up to watch the league match against Wigan in January 1949.

Fleming, 5ft 8in and 11st 6lb, was transferred to Widnes in January 1950 and played against Warrington in the Challenge Cup final at Wembley that May. He later returned to Wigan and had a short spell with Leigh in 1955 before beginning his coaching career.

Tommy Flynn
Stand-off, 1925-32

Season	Apps	Tries	Pts
1925/26	19	6	18
1926/27	38	22	66
1927/28	38	10	30
1928/29	44	14	42
1929/30	35	6	18
1930/31	30	12	36
1931/32	20	3	9
TOTAL	**224**	**73**	**219**

Flynn also kicked 42 goals and 7 drop goals.

Welsh stand-off Tommy Flynn and scrum-half Dai Davies must have inspired and irritated the Warrington side in equal measure. For four seasons, they formed one of the best half-back combinations in the League but, horror of horrors, they chatted to each other in Welsh – a language their team-mates could not understand.

Flynn arrived at Wilderspool first when he was signed from St Helens for £400 in December 1925 and quickly established himself in the team, scoring 22 tries in his first full season with the club. Davies followed in November 1927, when he moved from Broughton Rangers, and, five months later, the pair were involved in the Challenge Cup final against Swinton at Central Park, which Warrington lost 5-3 after bring reduced to twelve men by injury. As described elsewhere in this volume, Davies began the match on the left wing, but was switched to the scrum-half role when Billy Kirk was carried off on a stretcher.

Flynn was the Warrington captain in 1927/28 and was ever-present the following season, playing in all 44 matches. He also collected a Lancashire Cup winners' medal when the Wire beat Salford 15-2 in the final at Central Park in November 1929.

Warrington were blessed with quality half-backs at the time, with Flynn, Davies and Kirk in a constant battle for two positions, but Flynn won with 224 appearances followed by Davies (196) and Kirk (102).

While at Wilderspool, Flynn also earned a Wales cap, as a scrum-half against England at Huddersfield in 1931, and made 4 appearances for the short-lived Glamorgan & Monmouthshire county side. When his playing days were over, he continued to serve the club for many years as groundsman.

He had joined St Helens from Talywain and went on to make 122 appearances for the Saints, scoring 38 tries and 5 goals for a total of 124 points. He even inspired one St Helens supporter to write 'An Ode to Tommy Flynn'.

> Here's a health to ye,
> Now Tommy Flynn.
> Faster, and faster, and faster agin.
> Powerfullest pacer,
> Wid steps like a racer,
> The other team's lacer,
> Is our Tommy Flynn.

Phil Ford
Left winger, 1981-85

Season	Apps	Tries	Pts
1980/81	5	4	12
1981/82	32(1)	9	27
1982/83	28(1)	20	66*
1983/84	29	20	80
1984/85	16	4	16
TOTAL	**110(2)**	**57**	**201**

* Ford also kicked 3 goals.

Phil Ford was a brilliant and unorthodox winger from Cardiff Rugby Union Club who spent four fleeting years at Wilderspool at the start of a rugby league career that would bring 13 Great Britain caps and more than 200 tries.

Ford was one of the stars of the 1988 Great Britain tour to Papua New Guinea, Australia and New Zealand. Indeed, he scored one of the five tries the Lions notched up in their famous 26-12 victory over the Kangaroos at Sydney in the third Test.

He also knew how to enjoy himself. Andy Gregory, in his biography *Pint Size*, recalled: 'Most nights on the tour we ended up having to buy Fordy a pair of sunglasses, because his eyes went all bloodshot after a couple of pints, and we needed to sneak past coach Mal Reilly on the way back to our rooms.'

Ford made his Wire debut, aged nineteen, as a mystery trialist against Featherstone Rovers in January 1981, scoring Warrington's only try in a 10-9 victory. He was officially signed after the match and quickly adapted to his new code to become Warrington's leading try-scorer in 1983/84.

Many of his touchdowns were length-of-the-field, individual efforts, featuring mazy runs, which often turned expected defeat into victory. At Oldham in March 1984, for example, Warrington were losing 11-6 with ten minutes to go and defending on their own line when Ford collected a kick, slipped the opposition and sprinted 80 yards to score at the posts. Steve Hesford added the conversion and a late penalty goal to seal a 14-11 victory.

To balance the books, however, Warrington were forced to sell Ford to Wigan in February 1985 for £40,000, which, at the time, was a record fee for a winger.

Ford made just 15 appearances for Wigan, scoring 16 tries, before he was reluctantly transferred to Bradford Northern as part of the deal that took Ellery Hanley to Central Park. Successful spells with Leeds and Salford followed.

At Wilderspool, where it all began, he had played for the Great Britain Under-24 team in France in 1982 and, in 1984, won the first of his 10 Wales caps.

Mark Forster
Winger 1983-2000

Season	Apps	Tries	Pts
1982/83	2	1	3
1983/84	21	8	32
1984/85	27(1)	16	64
1985/86	34(6)	14	56
1986/87	27(1)	10	40
1987/88	22(1)	8	32
1988/89	16	5	20
1989/90	35(1)	15	60
1990/91	15	6	24
1991/92	9(1)	5	20
1992/93	24(4)	6	24
1993/94	32	12	48
1994/95	40	24	96
1995/96	18	10	40
1996	24	7	28
1997	28	12	48
1998	23	11	44
1999	31(1)	16	64
2000	14	5	20
TOTAL	**442(16)**	**191**	**763**

Forster also kicked 3 goals.

One of the reasons for Wigan's remarkable success over the years is the bedrock of local talent. Warrington have not been quite so fortunate, but in Mark Forster they had a wonderful example of a local lad who came through the ranks and graduated to full international honours.

Forster made his debut for Warrington's A team as an amateur while he was a pupil at Richard Fairclough High School and playing for Woolston Rovers. He was still a regular in the first team almost twenty years later.

Forster signed professional forms on his seventeenth birthday in November 1981 and made his first-team debut as a centre in a league match at Barrow in January 1983. Later that season, he scored his first try for the club, at Hull KR, when touchdowns were still only worth three points. Towards the end of his playing career, that fact would regularly be trotted out to prove just what a seasoned campaigner he had become. 'Everyone keeps reminding me of that one,' said Forster in February 1999. 'I don't know which reporter brought it up but I will have to have a word with him.'

Like all great wingers, Forster was fast. He proved just how fast in November 1986 when he beat all his rivals in the Whitbread Trophy Bitter Sprint before the third Test between Great Britain and Australia at Wigan. Forster's prize was a cheque for £1,000 and the knowledge that he was the fastest man in the British game.

Forster lost that particular crown when Widnes signed the frighteningly quick Martin Offiah, but he remained the fastest man at Wilderspool, with the possible exception of Des Drummond, until well past his thirtieth birthday.

By then, Forster was claiming to be the strongest man at the club and at 5ft 10in and 15 stones not many were prepared to argue with him. Increasingly, Forster used his strength to support his forwards and his

Try star: Mark Forster heads for the try line at Central Park, leaving Wigan's Mark Preston (left) and Joe Lydon trailing in his wake.

tremendous work rate was one of the reasons he was named the *Warrington Guardian* Sports Personality of the Year in 1997.

Primarily, however, he is remembered as a prolific try-scorer and his tally of 191 puts him comfortably in fourth place in the club's all-time list behind Brian Bevan (740), Jack Fish (215) and John Bevan (201).

He also had a knack of scoring important tries, including six in major finals. His most important try, however, was probably the one against Oldham in the 1990 Challenge Cup semi-final at Central Park, which sealed Warrington's return to Wembley after a gap of fifteen years. Forster latched onto a pass from substitute Mark Thomas and touched down in the corner for a regulation winger's try.

'I dislocated my shoulder at Wembley and Tony Rothwell, the physio, told me to come off the field,' Forster recalled. 'I said "No, it's taken me ten years to get here and I'm not coming off." So he actually put the shoulder back in at Wembley. As he was doing it, the BBC panned round and showed my face –

the language was choice! That injury kept me out for eight and a half months.'

Forster scored tries against every other Super League club, including 17 against Wigan and 15 against St Helens. He also made a point of scoring against Wigan in the annual pre-season Locker Cup games, including a hat-trick in the 1989 match.

Forster also played twice for Great Britain, 3 times for the Great Britain Under-21s and 2 games for Lancashire. He also represented Ireland, aged thirty-five, in the 2000 Rugby League World Cup, courtesy of an Irish grandmother, and scored one of his trademark length-of-the-field tries against the New Zealand Maori at Tolka Park, Dublin.

Following the tournament, he joined Widnes in the Northern Ford Premiership and was soon able to take his career try total through the 200 barrier – an impressive achievement for an impressive player.

Eric Fraser
Full-back, 1951-64

Season	Apps	Tries	Goals	Pts
1951/52	12	2	0	6
1952/53	6	1	0	3
1953/54	3	1	0	3
1954/55	11	2	0	6
1955/56	30	10	1	32
1956/57	40	9	4	35
1957/58	40	6	73	164
1958/59	33	3	99	207
1959/60	38	3	94	197
1960/61	37	6	103	224
1961/62	31	1	28	59
1962/63	21	1	10	23
1963/64	37	5	60	135
1964/65	13	0	1	2
TOTAL	**352**	**50**	**473**	**1096**

Eric Fraser was one of the greatest full-backs in the history of his club and his country and he played a leading role in one of the most famous matches in the history of the sport.

The date was 5 July 1958, the venue was the Exhibition Ground, Brisbane and the match was the second Test between Australia and Great Britain with the Kangaroos 1-0 ahead in the best-of-three series.

Prop-forward Alan Prescott, the Great Britain captain, broke his right forearm in the third minute but, in the days before substitutes were allowed, he refused to leave the field and played on for 77 minutes with his arm hanging uselessly by his side.

Stand-off Dave Bolton had to leave the field with a broken collar bone while Fraser (elbow), Jim Challinor (shoulder) and Vince Karalius (back) all suffered injuries which required hospital treatment after the game.

But Great Britain were inspired by the nineteen-year-old Alex Murphy and recorded a famous 25-18 victory to square the series, with Fraser kicking five goals. It was the stuff of which legends are made and after Fraser died, at the age of sixty-eight, in July 2000, Murphy's thoughts quickly returned to that distant day. 'Not only was he an excellent footballer but he was a gentleman who was very well respected in the game and will be sadly missed,' said Murphy. 'He was the last line of defence in one of the best games of rugby league ever played and he helped Great Britain win with a very bad injury. Eric was one of the best full-backs I have ever seen.'

Fraser toured Australia and New Zealand again in 1962 and scored four tries in a match against South Africa in Durban that August. He was better known as a goalkicker, however, and his best haul was 15 goals in a match for Great Britain against North Queensland during that 1958 tour.

As a teenager, Fraser had shown lots of potential at football and was invited to have trials with Manchester United. But after just one training session with them he was persuaded by his workmates to try his luck at rugby league with the British Legion team in St Helens, near his home in Whiston.

Fraser, who was 5ft 11in tall and weighed 13st 6lb, was a natural and was soon walking into Wilderspool and asking for a trial with

Winning team: Eric Fraser lines up for the 1954/55 pre-season trial game at Wilderspool. Left to right, back row, are: David Brocklehurst, Eric Fraser, Danny Naughton, Ted White, Laurie Gilfedder, Jim Challinor, Brian Bevan. Front row: Len Horton, Gerry Lowe, Albert Naughton, Frank Wright, Gerry Smith, Stan McCormick.

Warrington. He signed for the club, aged nineteen, in 1951 and made his Wire debut that October as a full-back, scoring two tries in a 29-5 victory over the now-defunct Liverpool City club.

After just a dozen first-team games, he was called into the Royal Navy on national service and, for two seasons, he played rugby union as a centre for the Combined Services at Portsmouth, travelling up to play for Warrington whenever he could get leave. On leaving the Navy, he spent most of the 1953/54 season in the A team as Warrington won through to the Challenge Cup final at Wembley and the Championship final at Maine Road.

Albert Naughton, the Warrington captain and centre, was then injured and Fraser was showing the sort of form to take his place until he, too, was injured the week before Wembley and the chance was gone. During the next couple of seasons, he played in the first team, either at full-back or on the wing, until in 1956/57 he established himself as the premier full-back at the club.

He was soon appointed captain and he led the team who won the Lancashire Cup in 1959 by beating St Helens 5-4 in the final at Central Park in front of a 39,000-plus crowd. Fraser also captained the side that lost 25-10 to a Lewis Jones-inspired Leeds team in the 1961 Championship final at Odsal in front of a crowd of 52,177.

His leadership qualities were also recognised by Great Britain and he skippered the national side to a 2-1 series victory over the Kiwis in November 1961. In total, he captained Great Britain four times and Warrington for five seasons.

Warrington granted Fraser a joint testimonial with Laurie Gilfedder in the 1962/63 season and he continued to be the first-choice full-back until he made his 352nd and final appearance for the club in November 1964.

Fraser was the first Warrington player to captain Great Britain and only Mike Gregory has managed to emulate him since. Gregory is also the only Warrington player to beat his record of winning 16 Great Britain caps.

Fraser was probably the greatest full-back ever to pull on a primrose and blue jersey. He will be long remembered at Wilderspool.

Eric Frodsham
Full-back, 1948-56

Season	Apps	Tries	Pts
1948/49	1	0	0
1949/50	0	0	0
1950/51	48	2	6
1951/52	24	2	6
1952/53	32	5	15
1953/54	48	3	9
1954/55	40	5	15
1955/56	33	2	6
TOTAL	**226**	**19**	**57**

Frodsham also kicked 34 goals.

Eric Frodsham stepped up to receive the Challenge Cup and the Championship Trophy when Warrington's greatest team completed the 'double' in the 1953/54 season, but he was not strictly the team captain.

That particular honour belonged to centre Albert Naughton who, unluckily, was ruled out of the last five matches of the season with a calf injury. So Frodsham was the captain for the drawn Challenge Cup final at Wembley, the never-to-be-forgotten replay at Odsal and the Championship final at Maine Road. It was a fitting tribute to the man who made the most appearances for the Wire that season, playing in 48 of the 49 matches.

Frodsham, who was born in St Helens on St Valentine's Day 1923, was the youngest of five rugby league-playing brothers. Alf and Henry played for Saints, Stan played for St Helens Recs and Rochdale Hornets and Arthur played for Lancashire Amateurs.

After spending four years in the Royal Navy, Eric signed for St Helens in 1947 but quickly fell out with the club. 'I went to work one Tuesday morning and one of the workers told me I was on the transfer list. I didn't know. I went home for my dinner and P.F. Ward, the Warrington director, was waiting for me and asked if I fancied going to Warrington and I said yes.'

That was the start of a glorious career, which would see the 5ft 9in full-back, who was a fearless tackler and fine positional player, appear in three Championship finals (1951, 1954 and 1955), a Lancashire Cup final (1950) and represent Lancashire.

The 1953/54 season was obviously the highlight, but Frodsham had already proved his durability by playing in every game in the 1950/51 campaign. He was ever-present again in 1954/55 before his career was ended by a serious wrist injury and Warrington, reluctantly, gave him a £100 pay-off.

'The best footballer I played with was Bryn Knowelden,' said Frodsham. 'The toughest player I played with was Ray Price. The best try-scorer was obviously Brian Bevan. The best forward was Harry Bath.'

Bobby Fulton
Stand-off, 1969-70

Season	Apps	Tries	Pts
1969/70	16	16	50*
TOTAL	16	16	50

*Fulton also kicked a drop goal.

Australian Bobby Fulton only made 16 appearances for Warrington between October 1969 and February 1970, but he made a lasting impression. When in 1998, the *Warrington Guardian* asked readers to compile their Warrington Dream Team, Fulton polled more votes than any other stand-off in the club's history. Welshman Ray Price, who was at the heart of Warrington's Challenge Cup and Championship double-winning team of 1953/54 and who won 9 Great Britain caps, was second.

So why was Fulton so popular with the fans? Firstly, he was an exceptional player whose arrival lifted spirits at a time when the club was in the doldrums. Second, he was from Warrington.

He was born in Stockton Heath in December 1947, but just as he was learning to walk his family emigrated to Australia and settled in Woollongong. So it was there that he learned how to run and how to play rugby league. Fulton learned so well that in 1966 he joined Manly, the crack Sydney club, and went on to become one of their, and one of Australia's, greatest players.

Fulton was the stand-off when Australia beat France 20-2 in the 1968 World Cup final in front of 54,290 fans at the Sydney Cricket Ground. So the sense of excitement when he agreed to guest for Warrington for four months in the 1969/70 season was perfectly understandable.

The 5ft 9in powerhouse, who combined lightning acceleration and huge physical strength, did not disappoint, forming a sublime half-back partnership with scrum-half and club captain Parry Gordon. Warrington were struggling when Fulton arrived but won ten and drew one of the sixteen games he was involved in.

Fulton was to play one more match at Wilderspool, the third and deciding Ashes Test in December 1973, when he scored the opening try in a 15-5 triumph for Australia. He returned to England as the captain of the 1978 Kangaroos and as coach of the 1990 and 1994 squads. Each time he returned home a winner.

Laurie Gilfedder
Centre, winger, back-row forward, 1951-63

Season	Apps	Tries	Goals	Pts
1951/52	2	1	0	3
1952/53	11	4	0	12
1953/54	0	0	0	0
1954/55	1	1	0	3
1955/56	3	1	2	7
1956/57	40	22	57	180
1957/58	33	16	76	200
1958/59	40	16	41	130
1959/60	42	9	39	105
1960/61	42	12	44	124
1961/62	38	8	90	204
1962/63	31	6	77	172
TOTAL	**283**	**96**	**426**	**1140**

Laurie Gilfedder became the youngest player ever to pull on the primrose and blue of Warrington when he made his debut as a centre, aged 16 years and 199 days, against Belle Vue Rangers at Wilderspool on 1 December 1951. Fifty years later, his record still stands.

He went on to accumulate 1,140 points for the Wire – to lie seventh in the club's all-time list – and win 5 Great Britain caps and make 9 appearances for Lancashire. His precocious talent was richly fulfilled. At 6ft and 15st, Gilfedder had the size, strength and speed to play anywhere in the three-quarters or back row. He could also kick goals. What more could you ask?

He joined the Wire from Warrington Rugby Union Club and, after completing his national service, was a giant figure in the team for seven seasons. He was the leading try-scorer in 1956/57, leading goalkicker in 1957/58, 1961/62 and 1962/63 and made the most appearances in 1959/60. Any club would want him in their team and, inevitably, he was transferred to Wigan in August 1963 with Warrington receiving a club record sum of £9,500.

In his four years at Central Park he continued to make headlines, notably in the 1965 Challenge Cup final against Hunslet at Wembley. Hunslet kicked off directly into touch and Gilfedder slotted home the resulting penalty from the halfway line to set Wigan on their way to a 20-16 victory.

He completed his career with two seasons under the expert eye of player-coach Alex Murphy at Leigh, during which he took his aggregate points total to a remarkable 2,315.

'The highlight of my time at Warrington was being picked for the 1962 Great Britain tour because I had just missed out in 1958,' Gilfedder recalled. 'It was the highlight of my career really. It was a fantastic trip. We were out for four months. We went to Australia, New Zealand and went on to South Africa and played three Tests there.'

Twelve months later, he joined Wigan. 'I was getting fed up at Warrington. One of the finest ball-players I ever played with was Nat Silcock and he emigrated to Australia in 1961. Then Warrington were undecided as to whether to replace him, so I asked for a transfer and they put me on the list.'

Brian Glover
Winger, 1957-70

Season	Apps	Tries	Pts
1957/58	5	0	0
1958/59	11	5	15
1959/60	0	0	0
1960/61	0	0	0
1961/62	32	11	33
1962/63	42	24	72
1963/64	25	14	42
1964/65	38	16	48
1965/66	35	16	48
1966/67	40	9	27
1967/68	41	15	45
1968/69	30	13	39
1969/70	33(1)	7	21
TOTAL	**332(1)**	**130**	**390**

Brian Glover would have been worth a place in any Warrington squad in any era. So could he be described as unlucky to be around in the 1960s when the Wire were struggling to recapture the glory days of the previous decade?

Glover, however, certainly does not see it that way. 'Looking back at my time with the club, the camaraderie is what sticks in my mind the most,' he said. 'It wasn't the money at all, it was all about winning a place in the first team and playing well. There was no fighting among the players. We got on with the job and enjoyed playing together.'

Glover's total of 130 tries puts him in tenth place in the club's all-time list. He also made 10 appearances for Lancashire between 1964 and 1968, scoring 4 tries. Yet for all his efforts, he only collected two winners' medals, for the 1965 Lancashire Cup final victory over Rochdale Hornets and for Warrington topping the Lancashire League table in 1968. He was also a member of the only Warrington team to win the Wigan Sevens, in 1965.

Glover, who was 5ft 9in and 12st 7lb, began his playing career as a hooker with Pilkington Recs, the St Helens amateur side. For one match, however, they were short of a centre and so Glover stood in and played well. Fortunately for Warrington, Albert Johnson, the former Wire winger, was watching and invited him for trials at Wilderspool. Glover quickly proved himself as a fearless and speedy winger who never took a backward step.

He made his debut at Oldham in September 1957 but, after only 16 first-team appearances, he was called into the army to do his national service and so missed the next two seasons. For most of the time he was stationed at Rhyl and kept fit by playing rugby union for Western Command.

He returned to Warrington's first team in August 1961 and stayed there for the next nine seasons. These days he is a proud grandfather and enthusiastic member of the Warrington Past Players' Association.

Parry Gordon
Scrum-half, 1963-81

Season	Apps	Tries	Pts
1963/64	11	2	6
1964/65	16	5	15
1965/66	35(1)	9	27
1966/67	37	13	39
1967/68	39	11	35*
1968/69	39	22	66
1969/70	35	18	54
1970/71	23(1)	6	18
1971/72	34	14	42
1972/73	30(4)	11	33
1973/74	45	15	45
1974/75	37(2)	10	30
1975/76	19	5	15
1976/77	32	9	27
1977/78	30(1)	7	21
1978/79	35	8	24
1979/80	28(1)	2	6
1980/81	2(5)	0	0
1981/82	1	0	0
TOTAL	**528(15)**	**167**	**503**

*Gordon also kicked a drop goal.

Parry Gordon's testimonial brochure in 1981 was simply called *Mr Loyalty*. It could not have been better titled. From October 1963 until September 1981, Gordon made 528 full appearances for Warrington plus 15 as a substitute. Only Brian Bevan has played more games and he was stuck out on the wing; Gordon, as a scrum-half, was right at the heart of the action.

Gordon's loyalty to Warrington can be traced back to the fact that, as a schoolboy, he was rejected by his hometown club, Wigan, before coach Cec Mountford persuaded him to sign for the Wire for £400 on his sixteenth birthday, 17 February 1961. Gordon was Mountford's last important signing for the club and what a parting gift he turned out to be.

Gordon was not noted for his kicking game, but he was quick and brave and an excellent support player. His speed and support play earned him a magnificent 167 tries for Warrington. Only four players – Brian Bevan, Jack Fish, John Bevan and Mark Forster – have scored more. His courage meant that, even at just 5ft 8in tall and weighing only 12st, he was always strong and reliable in defence.

Gordon quickly worked his way through Warrington's Colts and A teams before making his first-team debut at home to Barrow, aged eighteen, on 26 October 1963. Two years later, he was the first-choice scrum-half and remained so for the next fifteen seasons. Most years he was either Warrington's captain, leading try-scorer or player of the season.

His loyalty was tested to the full during the 1960s, however, as Warrington struggled to recapture the glory days of the previous decade. Then, on 29 November 1970, he was a member of the side who lost 50-0 at home to Salford, a defeat that still gives him nightmares. But salvation was soon at hand as Ossie Davies bought the club in 1971 and

Parry Gordon was described as 'the little man with the big heart' by his coach, Alex Murphy.

appointed Alex Murphy as player-coach. Murphy rebuilt most of the Warrington squad but in Gordon, full-back Derek Whitehead and prop-forward Brian Brady he found three players who were good enough for any team.

The good times started to roll at Wilderspool and Gordon appeared in eight major cup finals in the next eight years. Victories came in the Captain Morgan Trophy (1974) and Player's No.6 Trophy (1974) and Gordon captained the team which won the John Player Trophy in January 1978 by beating Widnes 9-4 in the Knowsley Road mud.

Gordon also played in two Challenge Cup finals at Wembley, collecting a winners' medal against Featherstone Rovers in 1974 and a losers' medal against Widnes twelve months later.

Sadly, on neither occasion, was Gordon able to give of his best. In 1974, he was injured in the first half and could not come out for the second, while in 1975 he had picked up a throat infection forty-eight hours before the match.

No matter, however. His reputation as a top-class scrum-half was already well-established, particularly after he scored five tries in one afternoon against Dewsbury, who were the rugby league champions at the time, in a match played at Wilderspool in March 1974.

Opposing scrum-halves certainly had the utmost respect for him. Tommy Bishop, of St Helens and Great Britain, said: 'Parry was an outstanding scrum-half, one of the best I played against here or in Australia. He was so sharp around the scrum and had a lot of skill. I never found it easy to get away from him and he was certainly unlucky not to get on a Great Britain tour.'

Roger Millward, of Hull Kingston Rovers and Great Britain, added: 'He was the complete scrum-half. It was impossible to take a breather against him. He was always eager to get on with the game and so sharp. His greatest asset was his competitiveness. One of the best scrum-halves I played against here or in Aussie – and a nice guy.'

Alex Murphy, meanwhile, described him as: 'The little man with the big heart.'

Gordon played 7 times for Lancashire and went on England's World Cup tour of Australia and New Zealand in 1975.

At Wilderspool, he also served as assistant coach to both Billy Benyon and Kevin Ashcroft before stepping down to spend more time with his wife, Val, and three daughters. His rare loyalty was also rewarded with two testimonial seasons. Both were thoroughly deserved.

Bobby Greenough
Stand-off, 1957-66

Season	Apps	Tries	Pts
1957/58	16	8	24
1958/59	37	27	81
1959/60	30	22	66
1960/61	38	30	90
1961/62	36	14	42
1962/63	31	20	60
1963/64	9	6	18
1964/65	23(2)	6	18
1965/66	9(1)	3	9
TOTAL	**229(3)**	**136**	**408**

Bobby Greenough was a Warrington stand-off who was fast enough to play on the wing for Lancashire and Great Britain. He made 8 such appearances for Lancashire, scoring 7 tries, and was a member of Great Britain's triumphant World Cup squad in 1960, along with Warrington team-mates Jim Challinor and Eric Fraser.

In the build-up to the 2000 tournament, the Rugby Football League tracked Greenough down to the remote Scottish island of Eday in the Orkneys, where he was building a house, and invited him to a celebratory dinner at which he was belatedly presented with a World Cup winners' medal.

Greenough had joined Warrington from the St Helens amateur club, Blackbrook, in 1957 and made his Wire debut at home to Salford that December. Greenough, 5ft 5in and 12st 6lb, was at stand-off and Alf Arnold was at scrum-half.

Very quickly, however, Greenough formed an exciting half-back partnership with Jackie Edwards and for six seasons they brought out the best in each other and out of Warrington. Without a doubt, the highlights were the Lancashire Cup final victory over St Helens in front of 39,237 supporters at Central Park in October 1959 and the entire 1960/61 season when, with Greenough contributing 30 tries, Warrington finished second in the league. They also reached the Championship final at Odsal, only to find Leeds stand-off Lewis Jones in imperious form.

In November 1962, Greenough was placed on the transfer list at £10,000 – the world record fee was only £11,002 10s – after missing training and failing to turn up for a match against Halifax. Player and club settled their differences, however, and Greenough and Edwards were back in harness the following April when Warrington suffered a heartbreaking 5-2 defeat against Wakefield Trinity in the semi-finals of the Challenge Cup.

Greenough continued to play for the Wire for another three years, making his last appearance as a substitute at St Helens in April 1966, by which time he had taken his try tally to an impressive 136. More than thirty-five years later, he still lies eighth in the club's all-time list of leading try-scorers.

Andy Gregory
Scrum-half, 1985/86

Season	Apps	Tries	Pts
1984/85	13	0	0
1985/86	32(1)	8	32
1986/87	13(1)	3	12
TOTAL	58(2)	11	44

Gregory also kicked 4 goals in 1986/87 and a drop goal in 1985/86.

The 1985/86 season is best remembered for Les Boyd's fantastic performance in the Premiership Trophy success against Halifax, but Andy Gregory was Warrington's player of the year. Week after week, match after match, it was little Andy Gregory – all 5ft 5in of him – who called the shots, made the breaks and set up the tries.

Gregory had joined Warrington from Widnes in a blaze of publicity in January 1985, just before the Challenge Cup transfer deadline. Warrington parted with transfer-listed forward John Fieldhouse plus an undisclosed cash sum and claimed a world record £75,000 deal. Officially, the world record was not recognised because the cash sum was not specified, but it soon became clear that Warrington had signed a world-class player.

Gregory, who was twenty-three, had been in dispute with Widnes and had not played since September and so it took him a few weeks to regain match fitness. Once he did, there was no stopping him. The highlight of Gregory's two years at Wilderspool was undoubtedly the Premiership Trophy run of 1986, when Warrington beat Widnes at home and Wigan away before thrashing Halifax 38-10 in the final.

Warrington and Gregory continued in that vein at the start of the 1986/87 season and Warrington were the Daily Mirror team of the month for November and December.

The 54-16 victory at Leeds on Sunday 16 November, with Gregory in outstanding form, was one of the greatest away wins in the club's history. Sadly, Gregory only played two more games for the Wire after that before joining Wigan, his hometown club, in a world record £130,000 deal in January 1987. Gregory had been listed at £150,000 – another record – a month earlier after being fined and suspended for missing training.

The fee helped Warrington report record profits of £60,792 that season, but Gregory was irreplaceable – as he proved at Central Park by helping Wigan to win 5 Challenge Cups, 4 Championships and 2 World Club Challenge matches.

He also took his tally of Great Britain caps to 26 before moving to Leeds and then playing for and coaching Salford. In 2000, he put his whole career down on paper in *Pint Size: Heroes and Hangovers* – one of rugby league's best autobiographies and an excellent read about an excellent player.

Mike Gregory
Loose-forward, 1982-94

Season	Apps	Tries	Pts
1982/83	17(2)	4	12
1983/84	29(6)	9	36
1984/85	23(4)	5	20
1985/86	19(2)	6	24
1986/87	27(1)	5	20
1987/88	28(3)	8	32
1988/89	25	2	8
1989/90	27	2	8
1990/91	7(1)	1	4
1991/92	8	1	4
1992/93	0	0	0
1993/94	12(5)	2	8
TOTAL	**222(24)**	**45**	**176**

Great players produce brilliant performances when it matters most and Mike Gregory could be relied upon to do just that for both Warrington and Great Britain. Nobody who has followed the fortunes of the national side over the past fifteen years will ever forget the magnificent try that 'Greg' scored in the epic third Test victory over Australia at the Sydney Football Stadium in July 1988.

The Warrington captain was sent clear by his namesake Andy Gregory on Britain's 25-yard line and raced 70 yards to the posts, pursued in vain by Kangaroo skipper Wally Lewis and loose-forward Wayne Pearce. The try sealed a famous 26-12 victory and gave international rugby league a much-needed shot in the arm.

Two years later, Gregory scored another important try at another famous venue when he touched down for Warrington against Wigan in the Challenge Cup final at Wembley. A minute before half-time, Gregory came storming onto an inside pass from scrum-half Paul Bishop to score at the posts and keep Warrington in contention at 16-8. This time he would finish on the losing side, but not before he had strained every sinew against his hometown club and created a second Warrington try for full-back David Lyon.

Gregory had joined Warrington from the Wigan St Patrick's amateur club in June 1982 and quickly established himself in the first team, collecting a Lancashire Cup winners' medal against St Helens in only his tenth appearance.

Gregory's enthusiasm on his debut against Huyton that September is still fondly remembered, with the eighteen-year-old tackling player after player, to the delight of team-mates and supporters alike. 'He was only a slip of a lad then,' recalled Warrington's coach of the time, Kevin Ashcroft, 'and had to do a lot of work on the weights to pile on the muscle but he did it superbly. In fact I can honestly say that Greg is one of the best trainers it has ever been my privilege to work with.'

Gregory had to wait four years for his next winners' medal, against Halifax in the Premiership Trophy success of 1986, but that Elland Road afternoon signalled the start of four glorious seasons for club and country. Gregory scored two tries on his Great Britain

Picture perfect: Mike Gregory flies in at the posts leaving a trail of Castleford defenders in his wake in the Challenge Cup tie at Wheldon Road in February 1984. This magnificent photograph was one of the National Union of Journalists Sports Pictures of the Year.

debut against France at Headingley in January 1987. The following February, aged twenty-three, he was appointed Warrington captain by coach Tony Barrow.

He was Warrington's only representative on the 1988 Great Britain tour of Papua New Guinea, Australia and New Zealand, playing in all five Tests besides scoring that try.

October 1989 was another special month, as Gregory led Warrington to victory in the Lancashire Cup final against Oldham at Knowsley Road and was named as Great Britain captain for the series against New Zealand. Like full-back Eric Fraser, the only other Warrington player to skipper the national side, Gregory led the Lions to a 2-1 series victory over the Kiwis.

The season ended with the Challenge Cup final at Wembley and with Gregory being appointed captain of the Great Britain squad to tour Papua New Guinea and New Zealand that summer. Once again, the Lions achieved a 2-1 series victory over the Kiwis.

Sadly, the non-stop playing schedule and 100 per cent commitment took its toll and Gregory spent more of the next four years on the treatment table than the pitch. 'If I'd been a horse they'd have shot me,' said Gregory in his testimonial brochure in the 1993/94 season.

A £35,000 transfer to Salford in August 1994 did not change his luck and so Gregory began his coaching career, as assistant to Shaun McRae at St Helens in April 1996. Two Challenge Cups and one Super League title swiftly followed. Gregory was appointed Swinton coach in April 1999 and is now on the coaching staff at Wigan with Stuart Raper and John Kear.

But it is as a young loose-forward in the 1980s, dedicated and enthusiastic, that Gregory will best be remembered by supporters of Warrington and Great Britain.

Iestyn Harris
Stand-off, 1993-97

Season	Apps	Tries	Goals	Pts
1993/94	10	4	19	54
1994/95	39	18	38	148
1995/96	22(1)	11	55	154
1996	18	4	67	150
1997	1(1)	0	3	6
TOTAL	**90(2)**	**37**	**182**	**512**

Harris also kicked 4 drop goals.

These days, Iestyn Harris plays rugby union for Wales at the magnificent Millennium Stadium in Cardiff and is well on his way to becoming a millionaire. His professional rugby career began in much more humble surroundings, however, when he was spotted playing rugby league for the Oldham St Anne's amateur club and signed by Warrington.

Harris, playing at loose-forward, was the star of the Warrington Under-19s team who won the Academy Cup for the only time in the club's history, beating Hull 19-12 in the final at Old Trafford in May 1993. Harris was still only sixteen, but it was already clear that the club had unearthed a tremendously talented back whose flair and elusive running could unlock the tightest of defences.

He made his Wire debut at home to Leigh that October, kicking four goals in a 24-6 victory, and matured so quickly that he was named Player of the Year and Players' Player of the Year for the 1994/95 season, when he scored 18 tries in 39 appearances.

Harris won his first Wales rugby league cap against Australia in October 1994 and was one of the brightest lights in the Welsh team that reached the semi-finals of the Centenary World Cup the following year. Jonathan Davies, who captained Wales at the time, was his mentor – and his biggest fan. 'It's hard to believe he's still only nineteen,' said Davies. 'I wish I had had that much talent when I was his age.'

Harris, in fact, was outgrowing Warrington and was put on the transfer list at a world record £1.35 million in July 1996 after a row with football executive Alex Murphy over his best position. Harris still went on the Great Britain tour to Papua New Guinea and New Zealand at the end of the season, playing in all five Test matches, but it was clear that his days at Wilderspool were numbered.

He signed for Leeds in a £350,000 deal the following April. Warrington received £325,000 plus prop-forward Danny Sculthorpe, Paul's younger brother. Harris was still only twenty and still improving. At Headingley, he was quickly named as captain and led the team to the inaugural Grand Final against Wigan at Old Trafford in 1998 and to two Challenge Cup finals – against London Broncos at Wembley in 1999 and against Bradford Bulls at Murrayfield the following year. He was also named the Man of Steel in 1998.

His £1 million move to Welsh rugby union in the summer of 2001 put a fair price on his talents, but was still a huge blow to the sport he had graced for nine seasons.

Gerry Helme
Scrum-half, 1945-57

Season	Apps	Tries	Pts
1945/46	39	14	42
1946/47	30	8	24
1947/48	44	16	48
1948/49	39	8	24
1949/50	41	5	15
1950/51	45	10	30
1951/52	41	9	27
1952/53	34	9	27
1953/54	37	9	27
1954/55	30	4	12
1955/56	41	9	27
1956/57	21	0	0
TOTAL	**442**	**101**	**303**

Helme also kicked 19 goals.

Gerry Helme was the first player to win the Lance Todd Trophy twice, as the man of the match in Warrington's Challenge Cup final victories of 1950 and 1954. Since then only two players have managed to equal his achievement, the Wigan pair of Andy Gregory (1988 and 1990) and Martin Offiah (1992 and 1994), and nobody has beaten it.

Like Gregory, Helme was the complete scrum-half and his partnerships with Jack Fleming, Bryn Knowelden and Ray Price were the springboard for most of the success Warrington enjoyed during the glory years of 1946 to 1956.

Helme had everything. He was quick, with a good pair of hands, he could kick with great length and pinpoint accuracy, his tackling was a joy to behold and his temperament and stamina were magnificent. In short, he was world class and his international record of 12 Great Britain caps and 5 England caps is testimony to that. He also played 11 times for Lancashire.

Helme was discovered when Warrington staged a number of trial games before the resumption of fixtures in 1945/46. During that first post-war season, he played at scrum-half (18 times), stand-off (19 times) and twice on the wing before making the number 7 jersey his own.

In the years that followed his long, raking kicks created many tries for Brian Bevan, but one of his tackling techniques, which became known as the 'Cumberland throw', was banned by the Rugby Football League. Helme, who was only 5ft 6in and 10st 10lb, used to grab the wrist of an oncoming opponent and, at the same time, duck under and down with the inevitable result that the opponent flew over Helme's back and hit the ground with a resounding thud. Opponents quickly decided not to use a hand-off when Helme was in their path.

Helme made a try-scoring international debut when England defeated Wales 11-5 at Wigan in September 1948. Later that season, he played in all three Test matches as Great Britain beat the touring Kangaroos 3-0 in the Ashes series. Inevitably, Helme was an automatic choice for the 1954 tour of Australia and New Zealand, playing in five of the six Test matches.

Catch me if you can: Gerry Helme escapes from a would-be tackler.

On his return to England, Helme was one of only three tourists selected to play for Great Britain in the inaugural World Cup in France and this proved to be his finest hour as an international as he helped captain Dave Valentine lead the team to victory. Helme even scored the match-winning try in the first World Cup final as the hosts were defeated 16-12 in front of 30,000 demonstrative Parisians at the Parc des Princes.

His finest hour for his club was the never-to-be-forgotten Challenge Cup final replay against Halifax at Odsal Stadium, also in 1954, which was played out in front of a then world record crowd of 102,569. Helme capped a magnificent display by again scoring the match-winning try in an 8-4 victory. It was nearly time for breakfast before some Warrington supporters reached home, in the long traffic jam stretching from Odsal across the Pennines.

While at Wilderspool, Helme also played in three Championship finals, emerging victorious in 1948, 1954 and 1955. Helme finally lost his place in the side to Alf Arnold in 1957 and was transfer-listed at his own request. He played his last game for the Wire at Workington on 2 February, and then went on to coach Leigh and Oldham. He died just before Christmas 1981 at the age of fifty-nine. Oddly, he passed away within hours of one of his greatest adversaries, Tommy Bradshaw of Wigan, who was sixty-one.

Steve Hesford
Winger, centre or full-back, 1975-85

Season	Apps	Goals	Pts
1975/76	22(1)	46	92
1976/77	30	122	244
1977/78	38(5)	155	310
1978/79	42	157	314
1979/80	35	122	244
1980/81	40	142	284
1981/82	33	110	220
1982/83	30	113	226
1983/84	35	135	270
1984/85	3(2)	4	8
1985/86	2	6	12
TOTAL	**310(8)**	**1112**	**2224**

Hesford also kicked 47 drop goals and scored 46 tries, taking his points tally to a club record 2416.

Steve Hesford was Warrington's greatest goalkicker, both in terms of the number of goals he kicked and in the reliability with which he kicked them. With his almost casual round-the-corner style, Hesford kicked a century of goals in eight consecutive seasons – an achievement which is unlikely to be equalled.

Hesford's best season with the boot was 1978/79, when he kicked 157 goals and 13 drop goals – for a grand total of 170 – to eclipse the club record of 162 jointly held by Harry Bath (1952/53) and Derek Whitehead (1973/74).

Hesford was to claim two more major club records before he was through. In January 1982, he overtook the career total of 834 goals that Cumbrian full-back Billy Holding had amassed between 1928 and 1938.

Two years later, he beat Brian Bevan's career points total of 2,288 with the second of his five goals against Huddersfield at Wilderspool in the first round of the Challenge Cup. Only Bevan and Hesford have scored 2,000 points for the club.

When Hesford was in his prime, Warrington could score fewer tries than the opposition and still win – as they did against Australia on a memorable Wilderspool night in October 1978. The Kangaroos scored two tries against one from Alan Gwilliam, but Hesford's six goals guided Warrington to a famous 15-12 victory.

Hesford was born in Zambia in May 1954, the son of Bob Hesford, who had played in goal for Huddersfield Town in the 1938 FA Cup final. Hesford, too, wanted to be a goalkeeper but he failed to make the grade with Preston North End before spending eighteen months playing soccer in Australia.

He returned home disillusioned and began playing rugby union for Fleetwood, where he was spotted by Warrington scout Albert White and offered trials at Wilderspool. It quickly became apparent that Hesford had the physique – he was 6ft 2in and 13st 7lb – and the goalkicking ability to be a formidable player. Hesford made his debut at Wakefield in November 1975 and kicked two goals as Warrington slumped to a 47-4 defeat, their heaviest First Division defeat at that point. Things could only get better.

At first, Hesford was pushed out on the wing

Three wise men: Parry Gordon (left), Steve Hesford (centre) and coach Alex Murphy at the reception after the 1978 John Player Trophy final. Hesford received the silver salver as man of the match.

while he learned what the game was all about and it was as a winger that he won the man of the match award in the 1978 John Player Trophy final. Hesford kicked three goals and launched the 'up and under' that led to John Bevan's try as Warrington beat Widnes 9-4.

That match came during a magnificent twenty-month spell from October 1977 to May 1979, when Hesford played and scored in 71 consecutive games – yet another club record and a tribute to his durability and talent.

The 1980/81 season was a triumph for Warrington and for Hesford. He collected a Lancashire Cup winners' medal in the 26-10 destruction of Wigan, scoring a record 17 points from a try and seven goals. He also found his best position when taking over as full-back after Derek Finnigan broke a leg in the drawn John Player Trophy semi-final against Castleford.

Two more winners' medals followed – in the 1981 John Player Trophy final against Barrow and in the 1982 Lancashire Cup final against St Helens. Hesford made his 300th first-team appearance in the spring of 1984, but his glorious career was then disrupted by knee ligament trouble.

'Steve Hesford is the Robert Redford of the team,' wrote John Bevan in 1983. 'If I had his looks, I would go into acting. What can you say about a man who has kicked 1,000 goals? He is the best goalkicker in the League and he has the safest pair of hands. A talker throughout the game with helpful advice to officials. Good player, should have had a game for Great Britain.'

Finally, in August 1986, he moved to Second Division Huddersfield for £8,000 but only managed two games and seven goals for the Yorkshire club before injury again intervened. All records are made to be broken, but Hesford's haul with Warrington looks safe for a few years yet.

Billy Holding
Full-back, 1928-40

Season	Apps	Goals	Pts
1927/28	6	5	10
1928/29	13	35	70
1929/30	37	84	168
1930/31	40	101	202
1931/32	33	92	184
1932/33	37	125	250
1933/34	42	116	232
1934/35	34	73	146
1935/36	26	67	134
1936/37	36	70	140
1937/38	19	60	120
1938/39	4	6	12
1940/41	1	0	0
TOTAL	**328**	**834**	**1668**

Holding also scored 6 tries.

Billy Holding was the first Warrington player to kick 100 goals in a season – and in an era when the ball was bigger, harder and heavier than it is today, that was no mean feat. Holding reached his century on the last day of the 1930/31 campaign, when he kicked two goals in a 16-0 victory at Leigh. He extended his club record to 125 in a season two years later.

Holding kicked some magnificent goals for Warrington, but none were more dramatic than the one at Central Park in the dying seconds of a third round Challenge Cup tie on a misty day in March 1933.

Wigan were leading 7-4 when Warrington scrum-half Dai Davies scored a try in the corner to level the scores with the conversion to come. Holding teed up the ball almost on the touchline and, with the help of some spectators, made a pathway through the straw which had been used to protect the pitch, to give himself an approach to the ball. The crowd fell silent as Holding ran up and toe-poked the ball, which sailed through the gathering gloom and between the posts. St Helens were beaten 11-5 in the semi-final two weeks later and Warrington were at Wembley for the first time.

Such was Holding's skill as a goalkicker that the publicity posters in London before the final declared: 'Come to Wembley to see Holding the wonder goalkicker'. On the big day, unfortunately, Holding could only kick four goals compared to six goals from six attempts by Len Bowkett, the Huddersfield centre, and so Warrington lost a thrilling final 21-17. Such is the lot of a goalkicker.

Holding, who was 5ft 9in and weighed 11st 7lb, arrived at Wilderspool from Maryport in Cumbria early in the 1927/28 season and played trial games for the A team under the name of Kimberley. He was quickly signed up and made his first-team debut, aged twenty, at home to York on 21 January 1928. He was the first-choice full-back and goalkicker for the next ten years, playing in five major finals.

He also left his mark on Wilderspool in another way. Along with hooker Nat Bantham and Welsh half-backs Tommy Flynn and Dai Davies (all ex-miners), he worked on the groundstaff and hollowed out

No try: Billy Holding appeals in vain to the referee during the 1933 Challenge Cup final against Huddersfield at Wembley watched by team-mates Tommy Blinkhorn (centre) and Bill Shankland. Stand-off Gwyn Richards' touchdown was given. Hudderfield's Stan Brogden (right) looks on.

the players' tunnel at some point during the early 1930s.

Holding collected Lancashire Cup winners' medals in 1929 and 1932 and was a key member of the Warrington team who suffered narrow defeats in the Championship finals of 1935 and 1937. He broke his leg in the first round of the Challenge Cup at Barrow in 1936 and that injury robbed him of a second appearance at Wembley.

Holding was granted a testimonial match in 1938, after ten years of exemplary service, and that raised the princely sum of £121/5/1. He was transferred to Rochdale Hornets shortly afterwards, but returned to Wilderspool in 1940 to make one war-time appearance as a guest player.

By then he had kicked 834 goals for the club, including four drop goals, to create a club record which stood until Steve Hesford bettered it forty-two years later, in January 1982. Not surprisingly, Holding was the first-choice full-back for Cumberland for most of his career, making 14 appearances which yielded 45 goals and a try.

However, in an era when he was up against men like Wigan's Jim Sullivan and Gus Risman of Salford – both founder members of the Rugby Football League's Hall of Fame – Holding was never able to realise his ambition of playing for Great Britain. He was, however, selected to play in the tour trials of 1932 and again in 1936.

When his playing days were over, Holding returned home to Maryport where he died, aged seventy-nine, in November 1986.

Bob Jackson
Prop-forward, 1984-94

Season	Apps	Tries	Pts
1984/85	28	3	12
1985/86	39	6	24
1986/87	38	10	40
1987/88	19(2)	2	8
1988/89	0	0	0
1989/90	22(2)	6	24
1990/91	17	1	4
1991/92	28	5	20
1992/93	16(1)	3	12
1993/94	15(1)	5	20
TOTAL	**222(6)**	**41**	**164**

Jackson also kicked 8 goals and a drop goal.

Reg Bowden's twenty-one months as Warrington coach are not remembered with particular affection by Wire fans, but he did get at least two things right. He persuaded winger Rick Thackray to return to Wilderspool after a spell out of the game and he signed Bob Jackson from his former club, Fulham. Jackson, originally from the Australian club Penrith, had only made 8 appearances for the Londoners after twice breaking an arm. But Bowden had seen enough to know that the twenty-four-year-old forward would be an excellent addition to the Warrington pack.

He quickly settled at Wilderspool and was the club's player of the year for 1984/85. That was only the start and the following season he took his place in one of Warrington's finest and fiercest front rows – Boyd, Tamati, Jackson – as the Wire lifted the Premiership Trophy.

Although hit by injuries, Warrington reached the Premiership final again the following season. Jackson was the acting captain and pushed Wigan's Joe Lydon all the way for the Harry Sunderland man of the match award as Warrington suffered a narrow 8-0 defeat.

Injuries eventually caught up with Jackson as well and he returned home in 1988 and missed the entire 1988/89 campaign. He was persuaded to come out of retirement, however, and the 1989/90 season would be the most memorable of his career.

Jackson scored two vital tries to earn the man of the match award as Warrington beat Second Division Oldham 24-16 at Knowsley Road to win the Lancashire Cup. Three months of inactivity with a back problem followed, but Jackson returned in style to help Warrington get to Wembley for the first time in fifteen years.

'Jacko' gave Warrington four more years of exceptional service and was awarded a testimonial season. Not surprisingly perhaps, Jackson was the first Warrington player to visit the blood bin when it was introduced at the start of the 1991/92 season. Jackson only lasted ten minutes of the opening match against Salford before he had to be replaced by another Australian, Don Duffy, and patched up. He returned to help Warrington secure a 22-20 victory.

Albert Johnson
Left winger, 1939-51

Season	Apps	Tries	Pts
1938/39	1	0	0
1939/40	8	4	12
1940/41	1	0	0
1945/46	19	9	27
1946/47	34	23	69
1947/48	32	19	61*
1948/49	25	19	57
1949/50	42	15	45
1950/51	36	23	69
TOTAL	**198**	**112**	**340**

*Johnson also kicked 2 goals.

Albert Johnson possessed the finest sidestep of any Warrington player before or since. One story, although probably apocryphal, illustrates the point wonderfully well. Picture the scene – Johnson is haring down the left wing at a packed Wilderspool, but is being rapidly closed down by the opposing full-back. The full-back attempts a tackle but, in a fraction of a second, Johnson has sidestepped out of reach, leaving the full-back to flatten the touch judge.

Johnson made his Warrington debut at home to Halifax in January 1939 and so his playing career was soon to be interrupted by the Second World War, although he guested for Wigan in 1943/44, scoring 15 tries in 24 appearances.

Johnson, 5ft 11in and 12st 7lb, won the first of his 10 England caps while with Wigan and was Warrington's only representative on the Great Britain tour to Australia in 1946, winning half of his 6 Great Britain caps. He also played 4 times for Lancashire. The first six seasons after the war saw Johnson in his prime and, with Brian Bevan on the right wing and Johnson on the left, the Warrington threequarters had pace to burn.

Johnson missed the 1947/48 Championship final victory over Bradford Northern at Maine Road with a leg injury, but took his usual spot on the left flank when Widnes were thrashed 19-0 in the 1950 Challenge Cup final at Wembley. He also played in two Lancashire Cup finals, against Wigan in 1948 and 1950. Both were played out before huge crowds at Station Road, Swinton and, on both occasions, Wigan won.

Johnson's career came to a tragic end when he suffered a broken leg during the 1951 Championship final against Workington Town in front of 61,618 fans at Maine Road.

He suffered the injury with less than 20 minutes gone and so, in the days before substitutes were allowed, the Wire had to play for an hour with twelve men. To add to Warrington's problems, centre Albert Naughton pulled a leg muscle and prop-forward Bill Derbyshire suffered a badly bruised shoulder. Not surprisingly, Workington won 26-11 and so, to add insult to injury, Johnson collected another losers' medal. To make matters worse, the broken leg was so bad that he never played again.

Johnson later served Warrington as a scout and spotted Brian Glover playing for Pilkington Recs. Glover, like Johnson himself, went on to join that select band of fifteen players who have scored more than 100 tries for the first team.

Johnson died, aged eighty, at his St Helens home on Wednesday 5 August 1998.

Brian Johnson
Full-back, 1985-88

Season	Apps	Tries	Pts
1985/86	27(2)	13	52
1986/87	39	25	100
1987/88	34(1)	10	40
TOTAL	**100(3)**	**48**	**192**

There are two reasons why Brian Johnson's club record of 25 tries from the full-back position during the 1986/87 season may never be broken. First, Johnson played in 39 of Warrington's 41 matches that year. These days, players feel hard done by if they have to play 30 games. Secondly, Johnson, who was thirty at the time, was a world-class talent at the height of his powers. He was quick, alert and timed his runs to perfection.

Johnson signed for Warrington from the Sydney St George club in September 1985 and quickly showed what he could do. In the Lancashire Cup final against Wigan at Knowsley Road, only his second game for the club, Johnson sprinted 70 yards from the base of a scrum to score the opening try. Wigan went on to win 34-8, but Johnson continued to impress and rounded off the season with another long-range spectacular, in the Premiership final at Elland Road, when he collected a kick near his own 25-yard line and sliced through the entire Halifax team. This time, his reward was a winners' medal.

Johnson spent the off-season playing for Eastern Suburbs, but returned to Wilderspool in record-breaking form. Unfortunately, some of his team-mates were not quite as talented and Johnson had to settle for losers' medals in the John Player and Premiership Trophy finals against Wigan.

A second Lancashire Cup losers' medal against Wigan followed in October 1987. By this stage, Johnson was helping to coach the Warrington backs and he was a popular choice as Wire coach when Tony Barrow resigned in November 1988. Johnson guided Warrington to two trophies, the Lancashire Cup in 1989 and the Regal Trophy in 1991, with a trip to Wembley in between. For such a gifted player, Johnson was a surprisingly pragmatic coach, but he kept Warrington at the forefront of the British game for seven years.

The 1993/94 season was another big success, with Warrington pushing Wigan and Bradford Northern all the way in a three-pronged race for the title. Johnson resigned in January 1996 after his team had suffered an embarrassing 80-0 defeat at St Helens in the semi-finals of the Regal Trophy. He deserved better.

Ben Jolley
Full-back, 1912-26

Season	Apps	Goals	Pts
1911/12	2	0	0
1912/13	38	6	12
1913/14	30	41	82
1914/15	32	19	38
1918/19	14	7	14
1919/20	16	23	46
1920/21	21	33	66
1921/22	28	51	102
1922/23	8	15	30
1923/24	27	23	46
1924/25	34	44	88
1925/26	30	53	106
1926/27	2	2	4
TOTAL	**282**	**317**	**634**

Jolley also scored a try and kicked 8 drop goals.

Full-back Ben Jolley was one of the stars of the Warrington team in the 1910s and '20s. Perhaps his finest performance came against Australia in October 1921, when he kicked all four goals as the Wire beat the Kangaroos 8-5 at Wilderspool in front of 16,000 delighted fans.

Five weeks later, another important career landmark arrived when his two goals helped Warrington to win the Lancashire Cup for the first time when Oldham were beaten 7-5 in the final at the Cliff – then home of Broughton Rangers and later to be Manchester United's training ground.

Jolley was also the first Warrington player to kick 50 goals in a season and, even now, seventy-five years after his retirement, his career total of 317 goals plus 8 drop goals sees him lying in tenth place in the club's all-time list of top kickers. Goalkicking, of course, was a much more difficult art in those days – the balls were bigger and heavier, the boots were less comfortable and the pitches were often mud heaps.

Jolley came from a rugby-playing family in Runcorn – two brothers also played for Warrington – and he made his Wire debut as a centre in a 9-6 defeat at Coventry in March 1912. It was not a good start.

The following season, however, Jolley proved his talent and durability by playing in all 38 of Warrington's matches and making the full-back position his own. He also kicked a goal as the Wire lost 9-5 to Huddersfield in the Challenge Cup final at Headingley.

Competitive matches were suspended during the First World War and, in the 1915/16 season, Warrington did not take part in the series of friendlies that had been arranged so Jolley, along with team-mates Jim Tranter and Jim Baker, went to play for Runcorn instead. Warrington realised the error of their ways and took part in the Merit Table games in 1916/17 and 1917/18, with Jolley making 30 appearances and enjoying his first taste of captaincy.

When competitive fixtures resumed, Jolley continued to lead the side for three more years and was awarded a joint testimonial season with Jim Fearnley in 1925/26. Each player received £203 7s 3d. While at Wilderspool, Jolley also won 4 caps for Lancashire.

Les Jones
Full-back, 1936-50

Season	Apps	Tries	Pts
1936/37	7	0	0
1937/38	16	5	15
1938/39	20	2	6
1939/40	25	4	12
1940/41	16	4	12
1945/46	37	4	12
1946/47	43	0	0
1947/48	42	1	3
1948/49	46	5	15
1949/50	18	1	3
TOTAL	**270**	**26**	**78**

Jones also kicked 7 goals and 14 drop goals.

Les Jones was one of the finest full-backs to play for Warrington. Affectionately known as 'Cowboy' because of his slightly bowed legs, he was Warrington's last line of defence for ten seasons and would have made many more appearances but for the Second World War.

Jones was the Warrington full-back when the Wire won the championship for the first time by beating Bradford Northern 15-5 in the final at Maine Road in front of a 69,000 crowd in May 1948. He also wore the number 1 jersey when Warrington thrashed Widnes 19-0 in the Challenge Cup final in May 1950 to win the cup at Wembley for the first time. Jones also played in two Lancashire Cup finals, collecting a winners' medal in October 1937 when Barrow were beaten 8-4 at Central Park and a losers' medal in November 1948 when Warrington lost 14-8 to Wigan at Swinton in front of a 39,000 crowd.

Jones, who was the Warrington captain in 1946/47, was the master of the kicking duels which were common at the time as opposing full-backs punted the ball up field in search of territorial advantage. He grew up in the Welsh mining village of Penygraig and played for the local rugby union club before joining Warrington as a teenager in late 1936. He made his Wire debut at home to Barrow in October 1936 – when the legendary Billy Holding was the regular full-back – and had established himself in the side by the time war broke out. Jones was a member of the Warrington side who were playing Broughton Rangers at Wilderspool in September 1940 when a German aircraft attacked the Thames Board Mills factory at Arpley Meadows, less than a mile from the ground.

After the war, he was one of the key figures in a revitalised Warrington side and played in the thrilling 1949 Championship final against Huddersfield at Maine Road when the Wire lost 13-12, despite a memorable fightback. Jones was dropped at the start of 1949/50, allowing Albert Johnson to play at full-back, but he was recalled for the onset of the Challenge Cup in February 1950, with Johnson reverting to the left wing. Jones played in every round, with the Wembley final marking the end of his Warrington career before he joined Liverpool Stanley.

Jones, who was 5ft 10in tall and weighed 12st, worked in a foundry while at Wilderspool. He died in January 1985 and a minute's silence was observed for him and his Wembley team-mate Ron Fisher before Warrington's game with Bradford Northern the following month.

Ken Kelly
Half-back, 1977-87

Season	Apps	Tries	Pts
1976/77	8(2)	2	6
1977/78	38	17	51
1978/79	34	10	30
1979/80	28	5	15
1980/81	39	12	36
1981/82	22(3)	4	12
1982/83	28	4	12
1983/84	36	6	24
1984/85	29	4	16
1985/86	23(1)	5	20
1986/87	16(9)	4	16
TOTAL	**301(15)**	**73**	**238**

Kelly also kicked 10 drop goals.

Ken Kelly, like all the best half-backs, was quick and clever and, most of all, brave. During his career, he suffered a catalogue of serious injuries – a broken jaw (twice), a broken arm (twice), a broken wrist, broken knuckles, a broken thumb and snapped knee ligaments – but each time he came back for more.

His first broken jaw, while he was still with his hometown club St Helens, meant he had to pull out of Great Britain's 1972 World Cup squad. His second broken jaw, while he was at Wilderspool, came three days before he was due to fly out with the Great Britain squad to tour Australia and New Zealand in the summer of 1979. Consequently, he only won 4 Great Britain caps – 2 with St Helens and 2 with Warrington – a scandalously low total for such a talented player.

After returning from his second broken jaw, Kelly enjoyed the most successful spell of his career. In 1980, Warrington coach Billy Benyon made him club captain in succession to Parry Gordon and he thrived on the extra responsibility. In the five years that followed, he led Warrington to Lancashire Cup wins in 1980 and 1982 and a John Player Trophy triumph in 1981. Also in 1981, he became the first Warrington player to be named Man of Steel and to be voted First Division Player of the Year.

Kelly's influence on the side was remarkable, as witnessed by one Challenge Cup tie at Castleford in February 1984. Warrington, with Kelly outstanding, built up a 12-0 lead thanks to tries from Mike Gregory and Ronnie Duane. Kelly then had to go off with a badly-bruised arm and Castleford went on to win 23-16.

Even after the captaincy had been passed onto Les Boyd and Kelly had entered the veteran stage, he still produced some superb performances. In the final of the John Player Special Trophy against Wigan in January 1987, for instance, he was once again Warrington's man of the match.

Two months later, he suffered snapped knee ligaments at Hull KR and needed a major operation on his left knee. While he was still hobbling around on crutches he suffered another body blow when his father, Jim, who had been his greatest motivator, died. Kelly never played for Warrington

Captain Fantastic: Warrington skipper Ken Kelly holds aloft the Lancashire Cup after the 16-0 victory over St Helens in October 1982.

again, although he remained at Wilderspool as A team coach until May 1989. These days, as secretary of the thriving Warrington Past Players' Association, he remains a regular visitor to the ground he graced for ten years.

At Warrington, Kelly was equally impressive at stand-off (217 appearances) and scrum-half (82 appearances). In his early days at St Helens, however, he was best known as a stand-off and it was as a number 6 that he collected a Challenge Cup winners' medal against Leeds at Wembley in 1972.

The following summer, St Helens bought stand-off David Eckersley from Leigh for a big fee and tried to convert Kelly into a centre. Kelly objected and was soon on his way to Bradford for a then club record fee of £11,000. Things did not work out at Odsal and he spent twelve months out of the game before Alex Murphy brought him to Wilderspool for trials.

Kelly broke his arm at Wigan in his fourth trial match. 'That was a real sickener,' Kelly recalled. 'I didn't tell anyone about the arm but went home. Later I phoned Alex Murphy up and said I would have to wait until it was mended, then have another trial. Alex said "Don't worry, we'll sign you anyway."' Murphy knew that a minor inconvenience like a broken arm was never going to stop Kelly from becoming a top-class player and a great clubman.

Warrington paid Bradford £6,000 and never regretted it. Kelly's efforts were properly recognised in November 1987 when he was presented with a then club record testimonial cheque for £13,000.

Billy Kirk
Scrum-half, 1927-34

Season	Apps	Tries	Pts
1927/28	12	2	6
1928/29	31	4	12
1929/30	16	4	12
1930/31	24	4	12
1931/32	3	0	0
1932/33	10	2	6
1933/34	6	0	0
TOTAL	**102**	**16**	**48**

Injuries are part and parcel of any sport but, mercifully, fatalities are rare. Many of the 12,000 Warrington fans who travelled to Wigan for the 1928 Challenge Cup final against Swinton, however, were convinced they had witnessed such a tragedy. Early in the second half, Warrington scrum-half Billy Kirk was concussed and play was held up for five minutes while he was treated. Eventually, he was placed on a stretcher and carried off the pitch.

Two men walking alongside the stretcher bearers were wearing shirts with collars and a rumour started that they were priests and that Kirk had been read his last rites and died. Warrington switched Welshman Dai Davies from the wing to take Kirk's place and Davies had a slightly different, but equally vivid, memory of the incident.

'I will never forget it,' wrote Davies in his autobiography. 'Billy was flat out and there was steam coming from him. He'd had a rabbit punch or something and he was steaming. There was a lot of fuss. Billy was a Catholic and so they brought the priest on. They thought he was dead. Then they carried him off and I had to come in off the wing and play half-back'.

Thankfully, the rumours proved untrue and Kirk, an honest, hardworking player with a strong defence, was back in the side early the next season. Kirk, a Wiganer who had been signed from the town's New Springs amateur rugby league club, even scored the first try when Warrington won the Lancashire Cup in 1929 by beating Salford 15-2 in the final in front of a 21,000-strong crowd.

Also that season, Kirk won an England cap against Other Nationalities at Halifax and made 2 appearances for Lancashire. He played his last game for Warrington in March 1934, before joining the now defunct Liverpool Stanley club.

Bryn Knowelden
Centre or stand-off, 1947-51

Season	Apps	Tries	Pts
1947/48	24	6	18
1948/49	18	5	15
1949/50	43	16	48
1950/51	39	10	30
1951/52	1	0	0
TOTAL	**125**	**37**	**111**

Centre, stand-off, captain and playmaker – Bryn Knowelden was all these things and more during his four years at Wilderspool. His 125 appearances included two Championship finals (1948 and 1951) and a Challenge Cup final (1950) when he scored one of the three tries as Warrington thrashed Widnes 19-0 at Wembley.

In his youth, Knowelden had been a keen football player until he was eventually persuaded to try rugby league. He took to the game so well that he was chosen to tour Australia and New Zealand with Great Britain in 1946.

Knowelden joined Warrington from his home-town club Barrow for £1,400 in December 1947 and quickly showed what he was capable of with a hat-trick of tries against Salford on his debut. Knowelden, at 5ft 8in and 11st 8lb, began his Warrington career as a left centre and made 57 appearances in that position. But he was an even better stand-off and played 65 times with the number 6 jersey on his back.

His first season at Wilderspool ended with Warrington crowned as champions for the first time in the club's history when Bradford Northern were beaten 15-5 at Maine Road. His best season, however, was 1949/50, when the signing of centre Albert Naughton from Widnes that November allowed him, then aged twenty-eight, to switch to the stand-off role for which he was perfectly suited.

Harry Bath was Warrington's victorious captain against Widnes at Wembley, but he began to feel that the responsibility was affecting his game and so Knowelden took over in December 1950 and led the Wire to the Championship final five months later. On the big day, nothing went right for Warrington with winger Albert Johnson suffering a broken leg after less than twenty minutes and, in the days before substitutes were allowed, Workington Town cruised to a 26-11 victory.

Knowelden was transferred to Hull Kingston Rovers at the start of the next season. The Challenge Cup final programme of 1950 had described him as a 'dainty and brainy player' – a fitting tribute to his Warrington career.

Toa Kohe-Love
Centre, 1996-2001

Season	Apps	Tries	Pts
1996	21(1)	9	36
1997	9(3)	4	16
1998	14	5	20
1999	33	28	112
2000	26	16	64
2001	21(2)	12	48
TOTAL	124(6)	74	296

When Toa Kohe-Love arrived at Wilderspool as a nineteen-year-old Junior Kiwi, few supporters had ever heard of him. By the time he moved to Hull five years later, he was one of the most sought-after centres in the game.

Kohe-Love's strike rate of 74 tries in 124 full appearances for Warrington compares favourably with the best in the business and he probably created just as many tries for his wingers. He did, however, have one serious flaw in his game: a tendency to concede penalties or, worse, get himself sent off for committing high tackles. Hull coach Shaun McRae is confident he can eradicate that problem and, if he is proved correct, will have a world-class talent on his hands.

Kohe-Love was snapped up from the Wellington club by new Warrington coach John Dorahy in February 1996. He was Dorahy's first, and best, signing, although fellow New Zealander Nigel Vagana would have to be a close second. Kohe-Love made his debut as a substitute at Leeds as Warrington opened Super League I, in March 1996, with an unexpected 22-18 victory. From then on, barring injury, he was an automatic choice in the right-centre position.

Injuries, including a snapped posterior cruciate ligament in his left knee, hindered his progress in 1997 and 1998, but in 1999 he was awesome, scoring 28 tries in 33 appearances and never missing a match. He never quite reached those giddy heights in the next two seasons, but still produced the occasional moment of genius, such as his try-making pass to winger Rob Smyth against Bradford Bulls at Wilderspool in August 2001, which sealed an 18-14 victory.

Kohe-Love, 5ft 11in tall and 14st, is a beautifully-balanced runner, with deceptive strength and a good pair of hands – qualities which earned him a place in the New Zealand Maoris squad for the 2000 Rugby League World Cup. His 74 tries for Warrington included four hat-tricks. He also scored against every other Super League club and will, no doubt, be looking to add Warrington and Widnes to that list shortly.

Allan Langer
Scrum-half, 2000-01

Season	Apps	Tries	Pts
2000	32	12	56*
2001	23	4	16
TOTAL	**55**	**16**	**72**

*Langer also kicked 4 goals.

Allan Langer had earned his nickname 'ALF' – Alien Life Form – long before he arrived at Wilderspool, but he certainly lived up to it with a series of performances which were simply out of this world. Warrington still struggled to achieve consistency on the pitch, but that could not be blamed on the 5ft 6in superstar from Queensland. His enthusiasm and love for the game never faltered.

The signing of Langer on a two-year contract in August 1999 and his immediate appointment as team captain was a spectacular coup for Warrington coach Darryl Van de Velde. Langer was thirty-three and had retired from Brisbane Broncos a few months earlier, but that short break had rekindled his appetite for playing.

He had starred in all four of the Broncos' Grand Final victories and had just been voted Australia's Player of the 1990s. He had also been on the Kangaroo tours of Great Britain in 1990 and 1994. In short, he was a legend and his eighteen months with Warrington left supporters with some magical memories. In fact, Langer's form was so good that Queensland coach Wayne Bennett recalled him, three weeks short of his thirty-fifth birthday, for the deciding State of Origin match against New South Wales in July 2001. Langer responded by producing one of the best displays of his entire career to inspire Queensland to a 40-14 victory in front of a 50,000 full house at the ANZ Stadium in Brisbane.

Langer's return to the primrose and blue of Warrington coincided with a humiliating 70-16 defeat at St Helens and from then on the pressure on Van de Velde became unbearable. The Warrington coach was told that the trip to Wakefield at the end of the month would be his last match in charge. Langer, as ever, rose to the occasion with the opening try in a 19-18 victory.

Langer immediately followed Van de Velde back home to Australia, citing a chronic ankle injury. Stories quickly began to circulate that Langer was unhappy with the way the coach had been treated. This may or may not be true, but one thing cannot be denied, Alfie Langer was an outstanding Rugby League player.

Dave Lyon
Full-back, 1987-92

Season	Apps	Tries	Goals	Pts
1987/88	22(3)	8	0	32
1988/89	29	2	0	8
1989/90	32	6	2	29*
1990/91	36	8	73	178
1991/92	25	7	37	102
TOTAL	144(3)	31	112	349

*Lyon also kicked a drop goal.

David Lyon was Warrington's first signing using the tribunal system and what a bargain he turned out to be. Warrington had offered £10,000 for the out-of-contract twenty-one-year-old; Widnes were seeking £20,000 and the tribunal, which took place on Tuesday 1 September 1987, valued him at £12,500. Five years later he cost St Helens £90,000 – a record fee for a full-back.

While at Wilderspool, Lyon, son of the former Wigan forward Geoff Lyon, worked hard to become one of the finest full-backs in the game. All his efforts, including some sessions with goalkicking guru Dave Alred, paid rich dividends.

Lyon was a member of the Warrington team who won the Lancashire Cup by beating Oldham 24-16 in the final at St Helens in October 1989 and he scored a superb try at Wembley the following April when the Wire lost 36-14 to his hometown club, Wigan. That summer, Lyon was further rewarded for his consistent season with selection as a replacement for the injured Alan Tait on the Lions tour to Papua New Guinea and New Zealand, scoring tries against Wellington and Taranaki. More success followed the following season, when Lyon kicked four goals in the Regal Trophy final against Bradford Northern at Headingley as Warrington won 12-2.

At St Helens, Lyon added a Premiership winners' medal to his collection, against Wigan at Old Trafford in May 1993, but made only 64 full appearances for the Saints because of injury problems. A brief loan spell at Sheffield Eagles followed in the 1995/96 season before Lyon switched codes, captaining his father's former club, Orrell, in 1996/97 – the first full season of professional rugby union. These days, Lyon is back in rugby league and on the coaching staff at St Helens.

Without doubt, the best days of his playing career were with Warrington, where he blossomed from a rather lumbering figure into a potent attacking player whose ability to punt the ball huge distances up the field also came in useful.

Lyon was also a member of the Warrington squad who won the British Coal Nines tournament at Wigan in November 1988 and played for Lancashire against Yorkshire in the Rodstock War of the Roses game at Headingley in September 1991.

Greg Mackey
Scrum-half, 1989, 1992-95

Season	Apps	Tries	Goals	Pts
1989/90	9	2	0	12
1992/93	33	4	4	29
1993/94	36	4	0	18
1994/95	30	7	0	31
1995/96	11(4)	2	0	14
TOTAL	**119(4)**	**19**	**4**	**104**

Mackey also kicked 20 drop goals.

Australian scrum-half Greg Mackey was described as 'the Little General' at Wilderspool because of his inspirational leadership and organisational skills. He was the captain of the Warrington side who came so close to lifting the championship in the 1993/94 season and reached the Regal Trophy final in 1995, only to be denied by Wigan on both occasions.

Mackey was also incredibly durable. From 30 August 1992 until 25 February 1995, he never missed a match, clocking up 98 consecutive appearances until he was beaten by a persistent shoulder injury. His run beat the previous record of 94 games in a row set by Steve Hesford between October 1977 and December 1979, but only tells half of the story.

Mackey's run of consecutive games actually started with his previous club, Hull, on 12 November 1989 and included 94 for them before his 98 for Warrington, making a grand total of 192, a truly remarkable achievement.

Mackey, who was 5ft 8in tall and weighed 11st 4lb, is also one of the select band of players who have enjoyed two successful spells at Warrington. He first arrived at Wilderspool in late August 1989 and played 9 games. Warrington won eight of them and drew the other, collecting the Lancashire Cup along the way. Mackey then received a lucrative offer from Hull and headed off to the Boulevard, earning the Harry Sunderland Trophy as man of the match when Hull beat Widnes 14-4 in the 1991 Premiership final.

Coach Brian Johnson brought him back to Wilderspool at the age of thirty in the summer of 1992 and was rewarded with three years of outstanding service. His record of consecutive appearances, for example, may never be broken and stands as a fitting tribute to his tenacity and superb level of fitness.

Bert Gordon, the long-time programme editor at Warrington, paid Mackey the following tribute: 'Ginger-haired, slightly built, extremely likeable off the field. On it, he showed courage, durability, skill, determination, motivation, leadership and, above all, that mental toughness which has pushed back the boundaries of Australian sport. Despite his attacking instincts, he frequently appeared as the last line of defence when others had failed.'

Duane Mann
Hooker, 1989-93

Season	Apps	Tries	Pts
1989/90	19(2)	1	4
1990/91	37(1)	7	28
1991/92	32	2	8
1992/93	33	10	40
TOTAL	**121(3)**	**20**	**80**

Mann also kicked 6 drop goals.

The duel capture of New Zealand internationals Duane Mann and Gary Mercer in November 1989 proved to be a masterstroke by Warrington coach Brian Johnson and chairman Peter Higham. Both players were to have leading roles as Warrington reached Wembley in April 1990 and lifted the Regal Trophy at Headingley in January 1991.

'The influx of Duane Mann and Gary Mercer has given us that degree of class which sorts the good sides from the rest,' said Warrington captain Mike Gregory at the time.

Like many great players, Mann grew up in a rugby league family. His father, Don, toured England with the 1971 Kiwis and his cousin, George, played for St Helens, Leeds and, later, Warrington. Duane Mann, who had a powerful 5ft 9in and 14st 10lb frame, took time to settle at Wilderspool but once he did, displacing Cumbrian hooker Mark Roskell, he was a revelation. Inventive from acting half-back, he seemed to pop up all over the pitch and he developed a talent for try-scoring.

From September 1990 to April 1993, Mann made 103 consecutive appearances which would have been a club record except for the fact that one of them – at Rochdale in February 1991 – was as a substitute. Still, the run was a remarkable achievement and a tribute to his fitness and endurance.

When the Auckland Warriors club was established, coach John Monie made Mann one of his first signings. In July 1994, the International Board Tribunal ordered the Warriors to pay Warrington £7,500 for Mann which was scant compensation for a player worth ten times that amount.

Mann was to make one final appearance at Wilderspool when, in October 1995, he captained the Tonga side who lost 25-24 to New Zealand in the Centenary World Cup after a pulsating match. Fittingly, Mann was voted the man of the match.

But, like many great players, Mann was his own harshest critic. 'I was pretty disgusted with my performance when Warrington lost at Wembley,' he admitted. 'The occasion was simply fabulous, but our performance was a huge let-down.'

Mann's cousin, George, a prop-forward, followed him into the Warrington pack in the 1997 season, making 17 full appearances plus 7 as a substitute.

Tommy Martyn
Second-row forward, 1975-81

Season	Apps	Tries	Pts
1974/75	16	6	18
1975/76	27	2	6
1976/77	34	10	30
1977/78	39	15	45
1978/79	37(1)	9	28*
1979/80	24	2	6
1980/81	42	7	21
TOTAL	219(1)	51	154

*Martyn also kicked a drop goal.

St Helens stand-off Tommy Martyn has formed a scintillating half-back partnership with Sean Long. Together they have won two Super League Grand Finals, a Challenge Cup final and a World Club Championship. Martyn also received the Lance Todd Trophy as man of the match when St Helens beat Bradford Bulls at Wembley in the 1997 Challenge Cup final and was voted the Super League Players' Player of the Year in 2000. But, as far as Warrington supporters are concerned, he will never be as good as his dad.

Martyn snr was the leader of the Warrington pack for seven years, during which time he also played for Lancashire and England and went on the Great Britain tour to Australia and New Zealand in 1979. He also collected winners' medals in the John Player Trophy in 1978 and 1981 and in the Lancashire Cup in 1980 – scant reward really for such a talented forward.

Martyn was one of the select few players with the ability to dictate and change the course of a game with his clever handling skills. Many young players burst into prominence at Wilderspool during his time with the club, feeding off his well-timed passes and gaining in know-how and confidence. Martyn, who was 6ft tall and 14st 8lb, was also a terrific tackler and a wonderful finisher when near to the line, as shown by his tally of 51 tries.

Martyn had played as an amateur with the Leigh Miners club before turning professional with Batley. He joined his hometown club, Leigh, in 1971, the season after they had won the Challenge Cup, but showed better timing when moving to Wilderspool in January 1975. Four months later he was lining up at Wembley as Warrington tried in vain to retain the Challenge Cup against a Widnes side who would quickly earn the nickname 'Cup Kings'. That summer, Martyn toured Australia, New Zealand and Papua New Guinea with Alex Murphy's England squad, making 4 appearances.

Warrington were entering a transitional period and were Premiership Trophy runners-up against St Helens in 1977 and John Player runners-up against Widnes in 1979. Martyn was magnificent throughout and was named as the Lambs Navy Rum Warrington Player of the Year in 1975/76 and was shortlisted for the First Division Player of the Year award in 1978/79, just missing out to Mick Adams of Widnes.

Tommy Martyn escapes the clutches of two would-be tacklers to score a try against Rochdale Hornets at Wilderspool in January 1977. Ken Kelly is the Warrington player backing up.

One of his best performances came against Australia on the memorable Wilderspool night in October 1978 when Warrington beat the Kangaroos 15-12 in front of 10,056 ecstatic supporters. Martyn made his second tour Down Under the following summer but, sadly, was sent home with a dislocated shoulder after playing in just five matches.

He was back to his best in the 1980/81 season, however, scoring a superb opening try straight from a kick-off in the Lancashire Cup final against Wigan at Knowsley Road when he caught the ball and charged 60 yards along the touchline to touch down in the corner.

Martyn was also the man of the match when Warrington beat Barrow 12-5 in the John Player Trophy final at Central Park.

Again he was shortlisted for the First Division Player of the Year award, this time being pipped by team-mate Ken Kelly.

By then, Alex Murphy – who had signed Martyn for Warrington in the first place – was back at Leigh and reclaimed his star second-row man in the summer of 1981. Again it proved to be an inspired move as Leigh won the Lancashire Cup and the First Division title during the 1981/82 season, with Martyn making 40 appearances.

If only Warrington had shown the good sense to sign his son as well!

Stan McCormick
Winger, 1954-56

Season	Apps	Tries	Pts
1953/54	16	7	21
1954/55	28	9	27
1955/56	4	1	3
TOTAL	**48**	**17**	**51**

Nobody has ever enjoyed a season quite like the fairytale one Stan McCormick experienced in 1953/54. McCormick was one of the greatest wingers ever to play the game. He was quick, he was smart and he could sidestep; when St Helens signed him from Belle Vue Rangers in 1948, they had to pay a world record fee of £4,000. That expenditure was justified when St Helens won the Championship final in 1953 with McCormick on the left wing.

McCormick began the 1953/54 season with St Helens and was a member of the Saints side who won the Lancashire Cup by beating Wigan 16-8 in the final. In January, he moved to Warrington with one major ambition still unfulfilled – to collect a Challenge Cup winners' medal. When McCormick made his Wire debut at Hull, Warrington lost 24-10. It was not a great start, but from then on the team swept all before them to complete the Challenge Cup and Championship double for the only time in the club's history. The signing of McCormick enabled Cec Mountford to move Jim Challinor from left wing to right centre and so complete what is arguably the greatest three-quarter line in the club's history – Bevan, Challinor, Naughton and McCormick.

The 1954 Challenge Cup final at Wembley was a sterile, unmemorable affair and ended in a 4-4 draw. The replay, by contrast, was one of the most amazing matches of rugby league ever played. What made it so memorable was the fact that it attracted a world record crowd of 102,569 to Bradford's Odsal Stadium. It was a titanic struggle, with Warrington snatching an 8-4 victory. Three days later, Warrington beat Halifax again, this time 8-7 in the Championship final at Maine Road, to do the double and McCormick was involved in one of the key moments of the match. Warrington were on the attack and the ball soon reached McCormick on the left wing. He cut inside and, in a planned move, kicked the ball across the field for Brian Bevan to run on to.

When the referee turned round, he saw Bevan collecting the ball and touching down near the posts. He disallowed the score, reasoning that no-one could run that fast. Bevan, of course, was disgusted because he could run that fast and knew that he had been on-side when McCormick had kicked the ball. Warrington retained the title the following season, but McCormick missed out on the Championship final against Oldham. No matter, he had already proved he was a champion with two different clubs. McCormick spent a spell on loan at Liverpool City at the end of his playing career and was the St Helens coach in the 1960s. He died, aged seventy-seven, in 1990.

Jackie Melling
Centre, 1963-71

Season	Apps	Tries	Pts
1962/63	1	1	3
1963/64	8	6	18
1964/65	32	15	45
1965/66	27(1)	7	21
1966/67	31	7	21
1967/68	37	21	63
1968/69	15	6	18
1969/70	12(1)	2	6
1970/71	8	0	0
TOTAL	**171(2)**	**65**	**195**

Melling also kicked a goal and 5 drop goals.

Jackie Melling was one of the Warrington stars of the 1960s. His finest hour came in the 1965 Lancashire Cup final at St Helens, when his two tries helped the Wire to a 16-5 victory over Rochdale Hornets. He was also Warrington's leading try-scorer, with 21 touchdowns in 37 appearances, in the 1967/68 season, when the Wire won the Lancashire League title for the eighth and final time.

At 5ft 9in and 12st, he was not big for a centre, but he was fast and that helped him win representative honours. In April 1965, he scored a try after coming on as a substitute for the England Under-24 team against France in Toulouse. He also made 3 full appearances for Lancashire during the 1965/66 season.

Signed by Warrington when sixteen, Melling matured in the club's Colts and A teams before making a try-scoring debut against Huddersfield at Wilderspool in April 1963. His final appearance was at Salford in January 1971 before he was transferred to his hometown club, Wigan.

On retiring, Melling became a highly-respected coach at the Wigan St Patrick's amateur club and returned to Wilderspool in October 1992 as the coach of Blackpool Gladiators.

Now aged fifty-seven and a local government officer working with a youth offenders team in Sefton, Melling has only happy memories of his time at Wilderspool.

'I enjoyed all the time there. The regret was that I never played under Alex Murphy. It was just coincidence that I packed in as he came along. It was sad.

'Winning the Lancashire League was better than winning the Lancashire Cup because it took a team effort over the season. That was my best memory and I thought it was our best achievement.

'I had been a football player on Bolton's books, but I just fell out of love with the game at the age of sixteen for some reason. I was in limbo, doing nothing. I went to school with Parry Gordon, and he just asked me if I fancied going down to Wilderspool and training. I went down, played a couple of matches for the Colts and they offered me terms.

'The team spirit was very good and my mind always goes back to 1967/68. I thought we were on the verge of having a really good team with a lot of young lads like Barry Briggs, Parry Gordon, myself and Ray Clarke.'

Gary Mercer
Centre or second-row forward, 1989-92, 2001

Season	Apps	Tries	Pts
1989/90	17	5	20
1990/91	35(1)	7	34*
1991/92	30	4	16
2001	18	2	8
TOTAL	**100(1)**	**18**	**78**

*Mercer also kicked 3 goals.

Gary Mercer's motto was 'train hard, play hard' and that simple philosophy earned him the respect of Warrington fans in three different decades. Mercer, 6ft 1in and 14st 3lb, first arrived at Wilderspool with fellow New Zealand international Duane Mann in December 1989. Aged just twenty-three, he had already won 12 New Zealand Test caps and been voted the Kiwi man of the series against Great Britain the previous month.

He was a class act and he already had experience of the English game with Bradford Northern, with whom he had collected a Yorkshire Cup winners' medal in 1987.

Mercer marked his Warrington debut, at Widnes on Boxing Day 1989, with two tries and he never looked back, helping the Wire to reach Wembley for the first time for fifteen years at the end of his first season. His first 22 appearances for Warrington were as a centre, but the signing of Welshman Allan Bateman, allied to his own appetite for hard work, resulted in Mercer moving to the second row. Indeed, Mercer was wearing the number 11 jersey when Warrington lifted the Regal Trophy by beating Bradford Northern 12-2 at Headingley in January 1991.

He continued to impress and was the only Warrington player to feature in the *Rothmans Rugby League Yearbook* Coaches Select XIII for the 1991/92 season as the Wire finished fourth in the Stones Bitter Championship. Leeds coach Doug Laughton had voted for Mercer and took him to Headingley for £90,000 in August 1992. Mercer spent six successful seasons at Leeds, returning to Wembley in the beaten sides of 1994 and 1995 and serving as Leeds captain in 1997 before moving to Halifax in 1998.

A spell as Halifax's player-coach followed, but when Mercer resigned from that post in March 2001, Warrington coach Darryl Van de Velde quickly signed him as a player.

Ming – as he is known, after the character in *Flash Gordon* – simply took up where he had left off almost ten years before with a string of wholehearted displays. His second try in his second spell for the club, against London Broncos in July 2001, was the 100th of his English career – an impressive milestone for an impressive player.

Jack Miller
Prop-forward, 1926-46

Season	Apps	Tries	Pts
1926/27	11	0	0
1927/28	38	1	3
1928/29	40	2	6
1929/30	42	5	15
1930/31	39	2	6
1931/32	35	2	6
1932/33	40	3	9
1933/34	37	3	9
1934/35	32	2	6
1935/36	38	2	6
1936/37	33	3	9
1937/38	40	1	3
1938/39	43	2	6
1939/40	20	2	6
1940/41	14	1	3
1945/46	24	0	0
TOTAL	**526**	**31**	**93**

Jack 'Cod' Miller earned his nickname by selling fresh fish as a door-to-door salesman. He earned his reputation as one of rugby league's hardest props by surviving for more than twenty years in the sometimes murky world of the forwards. He made his Warrington debut on 11 December 1926 as a chubby-faced youngster and, for a while, was looked upon as a bit of a clown.

By total dedication and application, however, he became a great prop-forward. Miller made his 526th and final appearance for the Wire against Kells, the Cumbrian amateur club, in the first round of the Challenge Cup on 9 February 1946. In the long and proud history of the club, only two players – Brian Bevan and Parry Gordon – have made more first-team appearances and they, of course, were both backs.

But even then, Miller's career was not over and he was transferred to Leigh, his hometown club, where he played another 25 games, including one at Wilderspool in November 1946 – when he was given a rousing welcome. Representative and guest appearances took Miller's career tally up to an incredible 651 matches, a figure which would have been even higher but for the disruption caused by the Second World War.

Miller, who was 5ft 8in and 14st 6lb, is the only Warrington player to have appeared in three losing Challenge Cup final teams – 1928, 1933 and 1936. He did, however, gain some consolation during the war, when he turned out for Huddersfield as a guest player and collected a Challenge Cup winners' medal after success in the two-legged final of 1945.

As well as his Challenge Cup disappointments, Miller also lost out in two Championship finals, against Swinton in 1935 and against Salford in 1937. He did, however, collect three Lancashire Cup winners' medals in 1929, 1932 and 1937. His involvement in the third success, against Barrow, however, was limited because he was sent off in the early stages as the opening scrum descended into violence.

Miller also played 6 times for Great Britain, 4 times for England and made 3 appearances for Lancashire. Along with his team-mate Sam Hardman, Miller was awarded a testimonial match in the 1937/38 season, after which each man received £135 10s. Miller died, aged seventy-two, on 23 October 1978.

Cec Mountford
Stand-off, 1952-53

Season	Apps	Tries	Pts
1952/53	26	5	19*
1953/54	11	1	3
TOTAL	**37**	**6**	**22**

*Mountford also kicked 2 goals.

Cec Mountford's place in the history of Warrington Rugby League Club is assured as he was the coach of the team who won the Challenge Cup and Championship double in 1953/54 – the only time the club have achieved the feat. Mountford, from Blackball, near Greymouth, New Zealand, was also in charge when Warrington retained the Championship the following season and won the Lancashire Cup in 1959. He was a master coach. Before that, Mountford had been one of the greatest stand-offs to play the game – quick off the mark, a brilliant organiser and a gifted leader.

He joined Wigan from the Blackball Rugby League club in 1946 and over the next five years he scored 70 tries in just 210 appearances. At Wembley in 1951, he became the first Kiwi and the first Wigan player to win the Lance Todd Trophy as man of the match in the Challenge Cup final.

Aged just thirty-one, he was still at the height of his powers when Warrington moved in and signed him as their first overseas coach on an unprecedented ten-year contract. Wigan were furious and retained his registration as a player. Mountford acted purely as Warrington coach for the 1951/52 season before Wigan finally relented, allowing him to resume his playing career in October 1952.

Over the next twelve months he made 37 appearances for the Wire, scoring 6 tries and forming an impressive half-back partnership with scrum-half Gerry Helme. He played his last game for Warrington in October 1953 before sitting back to admire one of his signings, Welshman Ray Price, take his place and form an outstanding combination with Helme.

When Mountford's ten-year deal expired he was offered a five-year extension which he refused to accept, demanding a seven-year agreement. The Warrington Board would not agree and so Mountford returned home.

His last major signing for the club was that of Parry Gordon. His last match in charge was the 1961 Championship final at Odsal, before a crowd of 52,000, which Warrington lost 25-10 to a Lewis Jones-inspired Leeds.

Mountford returned to England in 1970 as manager of the New Zealand World Cup squad and to Wilderspool in 1980, again as tour manager, when the Kiwis were beaten 11-7. In 1998, two former Warrington forwards, Alistair Brindle and Joe Whittaker, paid Mountford a visit in Australia. They found their former coach, then aged eighty, fit and well and living in a bungalow named 'Central Park'.

Alex Murphy
Stand-off, 1971-75

Season	Apps	Tries	Pts
1971/72	29	6	18
1972/73	20	2	6
1973/74	12(1)	1	3
1974/75	4	0	0
1975/76	1	0	0
TOTAL	**66(1)**	**9**	**27**

Murphy also kicked 12 goals and 28 drop goals.

Alex Murphy was past his breathtaking best as a player when he joined Warrington as player-coach in May 1971. He was, after all, thirty-two years old and had already achieved everything the game had to offer. But he was, however, still good enough to win his 27th and final Great Britain cap that October, in the second Test against New Zealand at Castleford's Wheldon Road. Mick 'Stevo' Stephenson, the Sky Sports television commentator, remembers the day well because he won his first cap, as a substitute forward.

In his pomp with St Helens from 1956/66, Murphy had been blessed with explosive pace but later, with Leigh and Warrington, he was still able to dictate play with his pinpoint kicking game, animal cunning and raw courage. Hence he remained a marked man, notably in December 1973, when a 'collision' with Tony Fisher, the Leeds hooker, left him with a jaw that was smashed in three places. Murphy, then thirty-four, underwent a three-and-a-half hour operation the following day and could have been forgiven for packing in playing on the spot.

Yet he battled back to fitness for the finest hour of his Warrington playing and coaching career, the 1974 Challenge Cup final against Featherstone Rovers at Wembley. Full-back Derek Whitehead received the Lance Todd man of the match trophy after kicking seven goals, but it was Murphy who had called the shots and landed two important drop goals in the 24-9 win.

The victory completed a unique hat-trick for Murphy, who was captaining his third different club to Challenge Cup success after St Helens (1966) and Leigh (1971). It was also his fourth winners' medal, starting with St Helens in 1961, and he was playing in his third different position – scrum-half (1961 and 1971), centre (1966) and stand-off (1974). He had also scored in all four finals.

Murphy remained as Warrington coach until May 1978 and returned as football executive to coach John Dorahy in 1996/97. Two years later, he received the OBE in the New Year Honours List for services to the game and, that May, returned to Wilderspool for an emotional reunion of the 1974 Challenge Cup-winning team of which he had been stand-off, captain and coach. There will never be another rugby league personality quite like him.

Albert Naughton
Centre, 1949-61

Season	Apps	Tries	Pts
1949/50	23	7	21
1950/51	43	26	78
1951/52	15	7	21
1952/53	27	17	51
1953/54	35	20	60
1954/55	36	26	78
1955/56	37	21	63
1956/57	29	13	39
1957/58	37	15	45
1958/59	14	4	12
1959/60	26	7	21
1960/61	26	4	12
TOTAL	**348**	**167**	**501**

Albert Naughton joined Warrington from Widnes in November 1949 for a world record fee of £4,600 and, over the next twelve years, he repaid that sum many times over. St Helens, in fact, had offered £5,000 for the twenty-year-old centre but Naughton wanted to go to Warrington and that was the end of the matter.

At Wilderspool he quickly established himself as a top-class player with great handling ability, pace and a stonewall defence. His first season culminated in Warrington's win over Widnes at Wembley – where he was in opposition to his brother, Johnny. Another brother, Danny, the Widnes prop, was on the slow boat to Australia with the Great Britain squad, but followed Ally to Wilderspool in December 1952.

Ally was a prolific try-scorer and his total of 167 from 348 appearances makes him easily the highest scoring centre in the club's history. He even scored five tries in a match once, at Belle Vue Rangers in March 1955. Yet he is best remembered for his devastating tackling. One tackle, in particular, against Halifax at Wilderspool, is still talked about. Johnny Freeman, Halifax's Welsh flyer, was haring down the wing, in full flight, about two yards from the touchline. Naughton, who was 6ft and 12st 6lb, looked to have mistimed his approach, but suddenly accelerated and hit Freeman round the thighs and took him into touch and right into the concrete perimeter wall another two yards back.

In the 1950/51 season, Naughton played in two losing finals, in the Lancashire Cup and the Championship, and his bad luck came back to haunt him in the 1953/54 campaign.

By then, Naughton was the team captain but he missed the last three weeks of the season through injury and was forced to watch from the sidelines as Warrington completed the Challenge Cup and Championship double. Like the great trooper he was, though, Naughton returned the following season to lead the team to victory over Oldham in the mud of Maine Road as Warrington retained the title. Naughton completed his collection of medals as a loose-forward in October 1959 when St Helens were beaten 5-4 in the Lancashire Cup final at Wigan.

He played his last game for Warrington, again as a loose-forward, in the team that lost to Leeds in the 1961 Championship

Mud, glorious mud! Warrington captain Ally Naughton raises the trophy after his teams' 7-3 victory over Oldham on a mud-heap at Maine Road in May 1955. His team-mates are, from left to right: Danny Naughton, Len Horton, Tom McKinney, Gerry Helme, Bob Ryan, Eric Frodsham, Syd Phillips, Harry Bath, Jim Honey, Jim Challinor, Brian Bevan and Gerry Lowe.

final. He still had no intention of hanging up his boots, but picked up a troublesome leg injury in the pre-1961/62 season trial game. Just when the leg appeared to be well again, he developed blood poisoning and was told to take a long rest. Finally, in January 1962, his doctor advised him to retire. It was a sad end to a glorious career.

Jack Steel wrote in the *Warrington Guardian*: 'A great clubman and a big-hearted player, Naughton proved of great worth to Warrington right to the end, for during the past two seasons he has helped out in almost every position whenever the Wire have been in a jam. In fact, he has played everywhere except the front row and scrum-half – what's more, he has always turned in a sterling performance.'

Naughton's representative career was equally successful and while at Wilderspool he earned 2 Great Britain caps, 3 England caps and made 4 appearances for Lancashire. The highlight of his international career undoubtedly arrived in Paris in November 1954 in the inaugural World Cup final. Naughton and Warrington team-mate Gerry Helme were both in the Great Britain side that beat France 16-12 in front of 30,000 demonstrative Frenchman.

On that day, and on many occasions for Warrington, Naughton proved he was a world-class centre.

Team-mate Eric Frodsham recalled: 'Ally was a good player, his record proves that. He was an all-rounder, strong in defence and attack. He and Jim Challinor were similar players and were ideal together. Ally was unlucky to miss Wembley in 1954 through injury. I was only the vice-captain, but I was captain then for all the big matches. I wouldn't have been if Ally had been fit. All the players respected him.'

Mike Nicholas
Second-row forward, 1972-80

Season	Apps	Tries	Pts
1972/73	16(2)	2	6
1973/74	26(2)	7	21
1974/75	13(3)	2	6
1975/76	21	1	3
1976/77	28(1)	1	19*
1977/78	13	0	0
1978/79	16(2)	0	0
1979/80	9	1	3
TOTAL	142(10)	14	58

*Nicholas also kicked 8 goals.

Thirteen was an unlucky number for Welsh forward Mike Nicholas, as it was the number of times he was sent off while playing for Warrington. Not that he was a dirty player, far from it, but he could look after himself and in the 1970s, when every pack seemed to contain an enforcer, that was important. Widnes had Big Jim Mills, Bradford had Jimmy Thompson and Warrington had Nicho.

His best, or worst, season was 1978/79 when he enjoyed an 'early bath' four times – against Featherstone Rovers, Barrow, Leigh and Bradford Northern. Also that season, he gave one of his finest, and bravest, performances in a Warrington shirt, against Australia at Wilderspool, helping the Wire to record a famous 15-12 victory. Tony Barrow recalls: 'Nicho had been out injured and was not expected to play but rolled up at the last minute and announced himself as fit. Billy Benyon said: "Right, you're in." What a decision. Nicho played his heart out, matching the Aussies blow for blow.'

Nicholas also gave an outstanding performance in the 1974 Challenge Cup final against Featherstone at Wembley, when he was a leading contender for the Lance Todd Trophy, and scored Warrington's second try. In many ways, that match was a turning point in his career because he also suffered a knee injury that caused him to pull out of that summer's Great Britain tour to Australia and New Zealand. It also cost him the chance of joining Manly, the crack Australian side.

Manly's loss was Warrington's gain and Nicholas was on the bench when the Wire returned to Wembley in 1975, only to lose 14-7 against Widnes. Warrington avenged that defeat in January 1978 in the John Player Trophy final at a rain-soaked and muddy Knowsley Road with Nicholas, by then in the front row, again outstanding.

Nicholas joined the new Cardiff City Blue Dragons club in August 1981 and went on to manage the Welsh national team and become chairman of the Warrington Past Players' Association. In 1999, he also organised a reunion of the 1974 Challenge Cup-winning team. Every player attended – if Nicho asked you to do something, it made sense to agree.

Derek Noonan
Centre, 1971-75

Season	Apps	Tries	Pts
1971/72	17(7)	8	24
1972/73	40	10	30
1973/74	43	9	27
1974/75	28	5	15
1975/76	12	2	6
TOTAL	**140(7)**	**34**	**102**

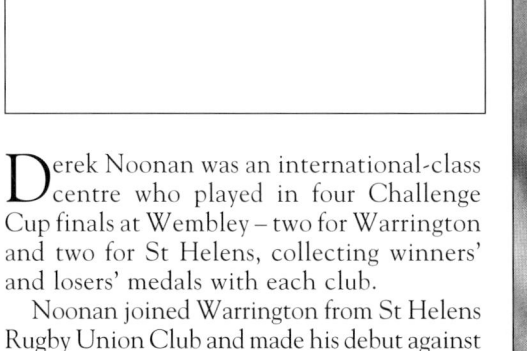

Derek Noonan was an international-class centre who played in four Challenge Cup finals at Wembley – two for Warrington and two for St Helens, collecting winners' and losers' medals with each club.

Noonan joined Warrington from St Helens Rugby Union Club and made his debut against Hull in October 1971. During his first two seasons at Wilderspool he alternated between centre, wing and stand-off. By the start of the 1973/74 campaign, however, he had made the right-centre slot his own, where his strong defence and tremendous attacking abilities were most effective.

Noonan was a member of the select group of ten players who appeared in all four finals that season as Warrington collected the Captain Morgan Trophy, the Player's No.6 Trophy, the Challenge Cup and the Club Championship. Noonan also proved himself as a player for the big occasions with two tries in the Players No.6 final against Rochdale Hornets and the match-winner against St Helens in the Club Championship final.

In November 1974, however, he suffered a broken jaw in a tackle by Robin Whitfield, the Huyton full-back who later became a referee, after only six minutes of a Players No.6 Trophy tie. The injury kept Noonan out of action for ten weeks, but he was back in plenty of time for Warrington's return trip to Wembley, against Widnes, which ended in a heartbreaking 14-7 defeat.

Noonan did not have much time to fret because he was off to Australia and New Zealand with England's World Championship squad, where he collected his third international cap to add to his 5 appearances for Lancashire.

But by the start of the 1975/76 season, Warrington's Challenge Cup-winning team was starting to break up and Noonan was transferred to St Helens, his hometown club, in a deal which saw scrum-half Alan Gwilliam move to Wilderspool. Four months later he was appearing in his third successive Challenge Cup final as St Helens demolished Widnes 20-5. He was back at Wembley again, against Leeds in 1978, but knocked on in the final minutes with the line at his mercy when a try would have given the Saints the cup. Nobody's perfect, but Noonan was very good.

Terry O'Grady
Winger, 1958-62

Season	Apps	Tries	Pts
1958/59	23	9	27
1959/60	36	22	66
1960/61	39	23	69
1961/62	34	28	84
1962/63	6	2	6
TOTAL	**138**	**84**	**252**

Once upon a time, Warrington had two wingers who had scored more than 1,000 tries between them. One, of course, was Brian Bevan. The other was Terry O'Grady. The pair reached the landmark during Warrington's 33-11 victory over Featherstone Rovers at Wilderspool in September 1961, when O'Grady scored five tries and Bevan scored one.

O'Grady had started his career with Oldham in the 1951/52 season and spent six years at Watersheddings that included a prominent place in the Great Britain party that toured Australia and New Zealand in 1954, when he was only nineteen. He joined Wigan in 1956 and was a member of the team who won the Challenge Cup by beating Workington Town 13-9 at Wembley in May 1958. Wigan, however, were well blessed for wingers, with both Billy Boston and Mick Sullivan on their books – and so in September 1958 O'Grady was allowed to sign for Warrington.

O'Grady, at 5ft 10in and 14st 5lb, was still a powerful player and four successful years at Wilderspool followed. He was on his usual place on the left wing when Warrington lifted the Lancashire Cup by beating St Helens 5-4 in the final at Central Park, Wigan, in October 1959 in front of 30,000 fans when he started the move that led to Bevan's match-winning try. He also played in the 1961 Championship final at Odsal when Warrington lost 25-10 to a Lewis Jones-inspired Leeds in front of a 52,000 crowd.

He was Warrington's leading try-scorer the following season, with 28 in 34 appearances. While at Wilderspool, he also played three times for Lancashire and once for Great Britain – in the first Test against New Zealand at Headingley in September 1961.

O'Grady played his last game for Warrington at Wigan in September 1962 and was finally released by the club in January 1965.

He had made 367 first-grade appearances, scoring 267 tries. He had won 6 Great Britain caps, 2 England caps and made 14 appearances for Lancashire.

O'Grady died in Bolton, aged just fifty-two, in January 1987, after watching Warrington and Wigan contest the John Player Special Trophy. Supporters and past players from both clubs were stunned by the news.

Harold Palin
Loose-forward, 1936, 1947-51

Season	Apps	Tries	Goals	Pts
1935/36	3	0	0	0
1947/48	34	10	77	186
1948/49	44	8	146	316
1949/50	43	8	132	290
1950/51	26	6	81	182
TOTAL	**150**	**32**	**436**	**974**

Palin also kicked 3 drop goals.

Harold Palin became one of the town's favourite sons after captaining the Warrington team that won the Championship for the first time at the end of the unforgettable 1947/48 season. He remains the only local lad to have led a Warrington team to victory in a major final.

Palin earned his nickname 'Moggy' as a teenager on the back streets of Warrington because of his cat-like agility. It was not a nickname he cared for, but it stuck and was already with him when he made his Wire debut as a full-back in a tough Challenge Cup second-round tie at Halifax in February 1936. Palin got his chance because Billy Holding, the regular number 1, had suffered a broken leg in the first-round tie at Barrow. The game finished in a 2-2 draw and Palin kept his place in the side for the replay, which Warrington won 18-15. He also played against Broughton Rangers two days later, but was then dropped and, feeling rather disillusioned, left the club and joined Swinton.

He served in the army during the war and filled out to a powerful 5ft 10in and 14 st. On the resumption of fixtures, he soon began to hit the headlines as a back-row forward and played twice for Lancashire in the 1946/47 season.

Warrington realised their mistake in letting him go a decade earlier and re-signed him from Swinton in August 1947 and made him captain. He quickly stamped his authority on the side and, against Wigan at Wilderspool that October, he scored 14 points from three goals, two tries and a drop goal as Wigan were thrashed 17-0 in front of 26,000 fans. Postcards were produced to celebrate the occasion.

Palin guided Warrington into the Championship final against Bradford Northern at Maine Road and, in front 69,000 fans, the Wire lifted the trophy for the first time with a famous 15-5 victory. Palin played his part to the full with three goals.

The following season, Palin was even more influential with a club record 146 goals and a club record 316 points as Warrington again reached the Championship final at Maine Road. This time, however, there was to be disappointment as the Wire lost 13-12 to Huddersfield in front of 75,000 supporters.

Normal service was resumed the following season, this time with the Australian Harry

Champions: Warrington's first Championship final-winning team was captained by Harold Palin at Maine Road in the 1947/48 season. From left to right, back row: Brian Bevan, Bryn Knowelden, Bill Riley, Dave Cotton, Bill Derbyshire, Albert Pimblett. Front row: Stan Powell, Les Jones, Harold Palin, Bob Ryan, Jim Featherstone. Seated: Jackie Fleming (left) and Gerry Helme.

Bath as the captain, as the Challenge Cup was collected following a 19-0 thrashing of Widnes at Wembley. Palin had a magnificent match, opening the scoring with a drop goal and giving the Chemics umpteen problems with his tactical kicking. He also kicked four goals to push Gerry Helme all the way in the voting for the Lance Todd Trophy.

The 1950/51 season saw Palin add another club record to his collection when he kicked 14 goals against Liverpool Stanley in a Lancashire Cup tie at Wilderspool in September. That record was Palin's alone for fifty years until Lee Briers equalled it against York in a Challenge Cup tie in February 2000.

Time was starting to catch up with Palin, however, and at the end of the 1950/51 season he was transferred to Halifax. Later, he played for Keighley but he was never forgotten at Wilderspool and when he died, aged seventy-four, in September 1990, there were even calls for the ground to be renamed in his honour.

While with Warrington, Palin won 2 Great Britain caps against New Zealand in 1947, playing a lead role in the 2-1 series victory. Palin scored two tries in the third and deciding Test, as Great Britain won 25-9 in front of 42,685 fans at Bradford's Odsal Stadium. He also won 3 England caps and made 3 appearances for Lancashire – against Yorkshire, Cumberland and Australia – and collected winning pay each time. He was a class act.

Alf Peacock
Hooker, 1919-29

Season	Apps	Tries	Pts
1919/20	21	0	0
1920/21	27	3	9
1921/22	38	1	3
1922/23	36	1	3
1923/24	43	0	0
1924/25	38	1	3
1925/26	40	1	3
1926/27	41	0	0
1927/28	38	2	6
1928/29	41	1	3
1929/30	4	0	0
TOTAL	367	10	30

Alf Peacock was Warrington's first specialist hooker and was easily recognisable on the pitch because of the skull cap he always wore to hide his balding head.

It was only after the First World War that clubs realised the importance of a regular number 9. Before that, players used to take up positions in the scrum depending on who got there first. It was under those conditions that Peacock played in every position in the pack with his previous club, Runcorn, before finding the role for which he was best suited. When Runcorn disbanded in 1918, Peacock joined Warrington, receiving a £7 10s 0d signing-on fee.

He made his Wire debut against Oldham at Wilderspool on the opening day of the 1919/20 season and hardly missed a match for the next ten years.

He was ever-present in the 1926/27 season, playing in all 41 of Warrington's matches, a sure sign of ability and durability.

Peacock was a quiet man, but he became an expert at his job. The team always enjoyed more than a fair share of scrum possession, especially in the early 1920s when he was flanked in the Warrington front row by Great Britain props Billy Cunliffe and Arthur Skelhorne.

In 1924, Peacock himself was selected to play in a Great Britain tour trial, which in those days was the hallmark of a good player, but, unfortunately, he missed out on the trip to Australia and New Zealand. Peacock was chosen to play for England against Wales at Wigan in September 1925 and made his only appearance for Lancashire that same season.

While at Wilderspool he played in four major finals, collecting Lancashire Cup winners' medals in 1921 and again in 1929. He was also in the Warrington teams that lost the Championship final to Wigan in 1926 and the Challenge Cup final to Swinton in 1928.

Many excellent hookers have followed Alf Peacock into the Warrington pack – men like Nat Bentham, Dave Cotton, Ike Fishwick, Kevin Ashcroft and Duane Mann – but he set the standards.

Lee Penny
Full-back, 1992-present

Season	Apps	Tries	Pts
1992/93	21	6	24
1993/94	33	9	36
1994/95	31	9	36
1995/96	21(3)	16	64
1996	15(1)	6	24
1997	19(1)	4	16
1998	22	8	32
1999	30(1)	12	48
2000	30	16	64
2001	18(1)	9	36
TOTAL	**240(7)**	**95**	**380**

Warrington have been blessed with some outstanding full-backs but none have scored as many tries for the club as Lee Penny. Penny scored on his debut, aged eighteen, against Blackpool Gladiators in the preliminary round of the Regal Trophy in October 1992 and has been on the scoresheet at regular intervals ever since.

He has scored tries against every other Super League club although Leeds, in particular, seem to bring the best out of him. At Headingley in June 2000, for example, Penny helped himself to four tries only to finish on the losing side – the first time a Warrington player had suffered such a fate.

Most of his tries have come as a result of some superb backing up, with his natural pace doing the rest. At 5ft 11in and 14st, Penny also has a strong defence and it was something of a mystery to most Warrington fans when, in the 2001 season, coach Darryl Van de Velde experimented with Penny on the wing and Alan Hunte, a former Great Britain winger, at full-back. Penny, a consummate professional, responded with seven tries in eight games before resuming the full-back role when Van de Velde returned to Australia.

Penny joined Warrington from the Orrell St James amateur club and signed his professional forms one Friday night in June 1991 at the home of the then chairman Peter Higham. The following morning, Wigan telephoned but they were too late. Penny had given his word.

At Orrell St James, Penny was in the same side as Andy Farrell, the future Wigan, England and Great Britain captain, and at one stage it seemed that Penny, too, would enjoy a glittering international career. He was certainly being groomed for the part and played 4 times for the Great Britain Academy side and won 3 caps for the Great Britain Under-21s in 1993. That, however, was the summit of his international career until he earned his first Scotland cap in 1998.

Penny – whose nickname is Jimmy – is now Warrington's longest-serving player and is working under his fourth different coach. He is also in his testimonial year and that select group of fifteen players who have scored 100 tries for the club are waiting for him to join. It should not take too long.

Barry Philbin
Loose-forward, 1974-78

Season	Apps	Tries	Pts
1973/74	16	1	3
1974/75	24	4	12
1975/76	5	0	0
1976/77	23(3)	6	18
1977/78	20	3	9
TOTAL	**88(3)**	**14**	**42**

Philbin also kicked 2 drop goals.

Barry Philbin was the final piece in the jigsaw for Warrington's all-conquering team of the 1973/74 season. He only made 16 appearances after being signed by Alex Murphy in January of that season but Warrington won every time, collecting three pieces of silverware in the process – the Players No. 6 Trophy, the Challenge Cup and the Club Championship.

Philbin, then twenty-three, was the man of the match in the dramatic Club Championship final against St Helens and so became the first Warrington player to win the Harry Sunderland Trophy. He seemed destined for even greater things but, tragically, a series of injuries were to blight what should have been the golden years of his career.

Philbin had joined Warrington from Swinton for £3,000 just before the Challenge Cup deadline and made his debut in the first-round tie against Huddersfield at Wilderspool. His second appearance saw the Wire beat Rochdale Hornets 27-16 in the Player's No.6 final at Central Park.

At Warrington he linked up with his older brother, Mike, who played on the right wing, and the pair became the first brothers to play in a Challenge Cup final team at Wembley when Featherstone were beaten 24-9 that May.

At 6ft tall and 13st 7lb, Philbin was not big for a forward but he was a good attacking player and strong in defence, qualities which helped Warrington beat Saints 13-12 in that Club Championship final. Philbin's good form continued the following season and earned him an England cap against France at Leeds in March 1975. He also made a return trip to Wembley with Warrington, but was not 100 per cent fit and was on the losing side against Widnes.

Philbin had been selected for the England squad to tour Australia and New Zealand that summer but was forced to pull out through injury. He eventually battled back to full fitness, however, and appeared in two more finals for Warrington – the 1977 Premiership final against St Helens and the 1978 John Player Trophy final against Widnes. The first was lost 32-20 on a sweltering May afternoon; the second ended in a 9-4 triumph in the Knowsley Road mud.

Murphy moved on to coach Salford at the end of the 1977/78 season and soon signed Philbin for a second time, but neither were able to repeat their Wilderspool heroics at the Willows.

Albert Pimblett

Centre, 1947-50

Season	Apps	Tries	Pts
1947/48	37	19	57
1948/49	37	12	36
1949/50	24	9	27
TOTAL	**98**	**40**	**120**

Albert Pimblett was Brian Bevan's regular centre and it was his job to take the heavy tackles and then get the ball away to the legendary Australian, whose freakish pace and unorthodox running would do the rest. At 5ft 11in and 13st, Pimblett was perfectly equipped for the role and that is why he was signed from Halifax in September 1947 for a 'big fee'. The following ditty dates from the late 1940s:

> Ball out, ball out, hear supporters call
> Scrum-half, stand-off, centre's got the ball
> Albert Pimblett is the call
> Give the ball to Bevan,
> He's the man to beat them all.

He made his debut at home to Belle Vue Rangers as centre to Bevan and both men scored tries. They were to develop into one of the most dangerous right-wing partnerships in the game and, by the end of the season, Bevan had scored 57 tries while Pimblett had touched down 19 times. They also produced the goods in the big matches, grabbing two tries apiece in the Championship semi-final victory over Huddersfield and a try each in the final against Bradford Northern. Pimblett's try sealed the victory. The following season, the Great Britain selectors recognised the vital role that Pimblett had played in Warrington's first Championship win and picked him for the three Test matches against Australia. Great Britain won all three, with Pimblett scoring four tries.

Warrington again relied heavily on the Bevan/Pimblett partnership – Bevan scored 56 tries while Pimblett touched down 12 times. The 1948/49 season, however, brought two big disappointments – a Lancashire Cup final defeat at the hands of Wigan and a Championship final defeat against Huddersfield.

The 1949/50 season looked like being even worse and the Wire directors decided that new blood was needed. Pimblett, who was thirty-one, and stand-off Jack Fleming were the unlucky men.

Pimblett played his final game for the club in March 1950 before joining Salford, but he is still remembered as one of Warrington's finest centres. He died, aged eighty-two, in May 2001.

It has been noted that Bevan sometimes gave his centres a hard time. On one occasion, when Pimblett had not given him many passes, Bevan told him, in no uncertain terms, that he would have been better off going to watch the horse racing at Haydock Park.

Ian Potter
Loose-forward, 1975-81

Season	Apps	Tries	Pts
1975/76	14(7)	1	3
1976/77	6	1	3
1977/78	35(3)	3	9
1978/79	19(1)	1	3
1979/80	7(2)	0	0
1980/81	29(4)	2	6
1981/82	5	0	0
TOTAL	**115(17)**	**8**	**24**

The *Observer* journalist Paul Wilson described Ian Potter as a 'strong and silent type capable of turning an average pack into an excellent one'. Potter was also a fitness fanatic who overcame a series of knee injuries to enjoy success with Warrington, Leigh and Wigan. Alex Murphy signed him for each club and each time Potter repaid his coach by becoming a vital component of cup or title-winning teams.

Potter was born in St Helens in August 1958 and, as a schoolboy, had trials with Blackburn Rovers and Liverpool, before making his mark with the Blackbrook amateur rugby league club. He joined Warrington in 1975 and made his Wire debut, aged seventeen, at Wigan that November. His progress was halted by injury in the 1976/77 season, but he made a triumphant return the following year and was a member of the Warrington team who upset the odds by beating Widnes 9-4 in the John Player Trophy final at Knowsley Road in January 1978.

Potter, who was 6ft 1in and 14st 7lb, collected a second John Player Trophy winners' medal against Barrow and a Lancashire Cup winners' medal against Wigan in the 1980/81 season. By then, Murphy was back in charge at Leigh and on the lookout for top-quality forwards. Murphy had to pay £50,000 to sign Potter in September 1981 – a world record fee for a forward – and received an instant dividend on his investment as Leigh were crowned First Division champions at the end of the season.

Murphy moved on to coach Wigan in June 1982 and signed Potter for £20,000 in February 1984. More success followed and Potter was one of three ex-Warrington forwards (Neil Courtney and Brian Case being the others) who lined up in the Wigan pack for the classic Challenge Cup final against Hull in 1985. Wigan won 28-24 after the teams had thrilled a capacity crowd by scoring five tries apiece.

While at Wigan, Potter also won 8 Great Britain caps to add to the Great Britain Under-24s, Lancashire and England appearances he had made at the start of his career with Warrington. Throughout his career, Potter was strong, silent and extremely successful.

Ray Price
Stand-off, 1953-57

Season	Apps	Tries	Pts
1953/54	38	7	21
1954/55	18	2	6
1955/56	35	10	30
1956/57	22	4	12
TOTAL	**113**	**23**	**69**

When Alex Murphy was still a schoolboy in St Helens his father, James, used to take him to Wilderspool to watch the Warrington half-backs, Gerry Helme and Ray Price. If Murphy junior wanted to be the best, he had to watch the best in action. Helme, as described elsewhere in this volume, was the complete scrum-half. Welshman Price, who was rugged, resourceful and a ferocious tackler, was the perfect foil for his talents.

Price, who was 5ft 5in and 11st 4lb, had joined Belle Vue Rangers from Abertillery in 1947. He moved to Wilderspool in August 1953, with Warrington parting with Great Britain forward Jim Featherstone and an undisclosed cash sum to complete the deal.

It proved to be an inspired move as the half-back pairing of Helme and Price was at the heart of the Warrington team who completed the Challenge Cup and Championship double that season. Not surprisingly, the pair were also chosen for the Great Britain tour of Australia and New Zealand in 1954.

During one of the club games on the tour, Price was the victim of a late tackle and promptly let his opponent have a left hook. The pair ended up fighting on the ground and a supporter ran on the pitch and kicked Price in the head. One of his ears was partly torn off and had to be sewn back on. Price was asked if he would recognise the fan again. 'I didn't see his face,' joked Price, 'but I would recognise the boot anywhere.'

Price was injured when Warrington retained the title against Oldham in 1955 but returned to the team in style for the 1955/56 campaign, scoring 10 tries in 35 matches. While at Wilderspool, he won 9 Great Britain caps and made 2 appearances for Wales and 2 for Other Nationalities.

He was transferred to St Helens in the summer of 1957 where, of course, he became Murphy's half-back partner. The master and the pupil were combined.

When his playing days were over, Price returned home to Blaina and one of his Great Britain shirts was on display in the local rugby club. He died, aged sixty-four, at home in 1988 after suffering a brain haemorrhage.

Mark Roberts
Second-row forward, 1984-89

Season	Apps	Tries	Pts
1983/84	0(1)	1	4
1984/85	15(1)	5	20
1985/86	21(6)	5	20
1986/87	29(2)	15	60
1987/88	29(3)	13	52
1988/89	21(2)	12	48
1989/90	3	0	0
TOTAL	**118(15)**	**51**	**204**

One of Warrington's greatest away wins was the 54-16 victory over Leeds at Headingley in November 1986. It was a terrific team performance but two men, in particular, stood out – scrum-half Andy Gregory and second-row forward Mark Roberts.

Gregory created most of Warrington's twelve tries while Roberts scored three of them to confirm his status as a top-class running forward who combined pace and power. International honours seemed certain but, sadly, injuries forced him to retire from the game in 1989 while he was still only twenty-five.

Roberts had joined Warrington from the Oldham St Annes amateur club in August 1983 after a successful BARLA (British Amateur Rugby League Association) tour to Australia. He quickly learnt his trade in the Warrington A team and made a try-scoring first-team debut as a substitute at St Helens in March 1984. His excellent progress continued until early in the 1985/86 season, when he started to tire during the latter stages of matches.

He was diagnosed as suffering from diabetes, but quickly accepted the situation and got the condition under control – so much so that he was one of the stars of the side who swept to victory in the 1986 Premiership final against Halifax. Roberts appeared in three more major finals for Warrington in 1987 – the John Player Special Trophy, the Premiership (when he played hooker) and the Lancashire Cup. On each occasion, Warrington were up against a Wigan team packed with internationals and had to settle for runners-up medals.

Roberts, however, was a member of the Wire squad who won the British Coal Nines tournament at Central Park in November 1988, defeating St Helens, Wigan and a Rest of the World team to claim the title.

While at Wilderspool, Roberts also played twice for Lancashire and for the Rugby League Chairman's XIII against Auckland when, in a typical example of his luck, he had to leave the field after 59 minutes with a suspected broken nose.

Roberts' career promised and, indeed, delivered so much – but could have been even more successful.

Bob Ryan
Second-row forward, 1945-58

Season	Apps	Tries	Pts
1945/46	29	2	6
1946/47	39	2	6
1947/48	44	4	12
1948/49	6	0	0
1949/50	29	2	6
1950/51	29	1	3
1951/52	35	4	12
1952/53	39	7	21
1953/54	43	7	21
1954/55	30	4	12
1955/56	34	4	12
1956/57	6	0	0
1957/58	9	0	0
TOTAL	**372**	**37**	**111**

Australian star Harry Bath rated Bob Ryan as the best second-row forward he ever played with. Ryan was not a big man in stature but in every other way he was a giant, with an abundance of strength and stamina. Those qualities earned him 5 Great Britain caps, 2 England caps and saw him selected for Lancashire 4 times.

Ryan was a Wiganer who learned his rugby at school and with the Platt Lane and Ince Rovers amateur clubs. In 1945, he reported to Central Park and played half a trial game. The Wigan chairman told him to get changed and that he would be down to see him later. Ryan waited until his patience ran out and he went home. He was then invited to play trials at Warrington and was quickly signed up as an amateur for a fee of 10s per match. He completed his professional forms during the first post-war season.

Ryan was a cornerstone of the Warrington team who won the Championship for the first time in 1947/48. After breaking a leg in August 1948, he returned fit and refreshed in 1949/50 and helped Warrington reach Wembley for the first time in fourteen years. Unfortunately, Ryan and team-mate Jim Featherstone had to miss the final against Widnes because they were with the Great Britain party heading for Australia and New Zealand. In Australia, Ryan played in the first Test which Great Britain won 6-4. Surprisingly, he was left out of the next two Tests, both of which Australia won to regain the Ashes after thirty years. Vic Hey, the Australian coach, said that leaving Ryan out of those two games cost Britain the series.

Back in England, Ryan was a major player in Warrington's best ever season, the unforgettable 1953/54 campaign when they achieved the Challenge Cup and Championship double. Now playing at loose-forward, Ryan at last got to play at Wembley in the drawn Challenge Cup final against Halifax. He was devastated at not having won, but what a replay it turned out to be with a world record crowd of 102,569 seeing Warrington win a thrilling match 8-4.

Three days later, Ryan helped Warrington complete the double by beating Halifax 8-7 in the Championship final. He was also a key figure in the team who retained the Championship the following season by beating Oldham in the final. Time was starting to catch up with Ryan, however, and rather than moving into the front row to prolong his career, he decided to retire in 1958 after 372 first-team appearances. Wigan's loss was most certainly Warrington's gain.

Ron Ryder
Centre, 1949-54

Season	Apps	Tries	Pts
1948/49	4	1	3
1949/50	32	16	48
1950/51	43	20	60
1951/52	26	6	18
1952/53	34	7	21
1953/54	22	1	3
TOTAL	**161**	**51**	**153**

Ron Ryder's Warrington career brought him two Challenge Cup winners' medals, one Championship winners' medal and a Great Britain cap. Not a bad haul for a player who some pundits considered too small to be a top-class centre. Ryder was only 5ft 7in and weighed just 11 stones, but he was fast – and that was the secret of his success and of his impressive right-wing partnership with Brian Bevan.

Ryder's father, Freddie, had been the Warrington captain in the mid-1920s and was on the coaching staff when Ron joined the Wire from Latchford Albion in 1949. That, however, did not make it any easier for the twenty-four-year-old bricklayer.

He made his Wire debut in April 1949, playing four games in nine days as a stand-off. But it was not until January 1950 when he wrested the number 3 jersey from Albert Pimblett that he made a first-team place his own. He scored tries in the first three rounds of the Challenge Cup that year and in the final, when Widnes were thrashed 19-0 at Wembley.

Ryder continued in that vein in the 1950/51 season, scoring 20 tries in 43 appearances, as Warrington finished top of the Northern Rugby League table. He never quite recaptured that form, however, although he was to be a vital member of the first-team squad for three more seasons, filling in at left centre, stand-off and even on the wing.

He was a surprise choice for the Great Britain side to face Australia in the first Test at Headingley in October 1952. Ryder repaid the selectors' faith in him by having a fine game and scoring a try in a 19-6 victory.

He played centre to Bevan for the 68th and final time against Bramley in the Challenge Cup first round, second-leg tie in February 1954 before losing his place to the nineteen-year-old Jim Challinor. That was his last game for two and a half months until after the drawn Challenge Cup final at Wembley, when coach Cec Mountford brought him back into the side for his big-match experience.

Ryder will never forget his last three games for Warrington – the Championship semi-final against St Helens, the Challenge Cup final replay against Halifax and the Championship final, also against Halifax. Three victories, two winners' medals and a game played out before a world record crowd of 102,569 meant that he had signed off in some style.

That summer, aged twenty-nine, Ryder was transferred to the newly-formed Blackpool Borough club and later became their coach. Good things do come in small packages.

Paul Sculthorpe
Loose-forward, 1995-97

Season	Apps	Tries	Pts
1994/95	0(6)	2	9*
1995/96	16(4)	7	28
1996	24	5	20
1997	28	3	12
TOTAL	**68(10)**	**17**	**69**

*Sculthorpe also kicked a drop goal.

Warrington fans did not know whether to laugh or cry when Paul Sculthorpe scored 30 points against the Wolves for St Helens in an embarrassing 70-16 defeat at Knowsley Road in July 2001. Sculthorpe's two tries and 11 goals from 12 attempts simply confirmed his emergence as a world-class talent, a fact that had been increasingly obvious from his days as a teenager at Wilderspool.

Sculthorpe had been spotted in 1992 playing for the Oldham junior side Waterhead, aged fourteen. Even then it seemed that he had a great chance of going on to play at the highest level and so he and his family were given the red-carpet treatment at Wilderspool. He officially signed for Warrington in October 1994 but, clearly, the deal had been done long before then.

Sculthorpe made his first-team debut aged seventeen as a substitute at home to Salford in March 1995 and he quickly became a regular in the side. His athletic 6ft 3in and 15st frame, combined with his deft handling skills, made it impossible to leave him out. He truly came of age in 1996, when he played in every game and was named as the *Warrington Guardian* Sports Personality of the Year – and he was still only eighteen. He did not celebrate his nineteenth birthday until the end-of-season tour of Papua New Guinea, Fiji and New Zealand, during which he won his first 5 Great Britain caps.

He continued to impress in 1997 and was appointed Warrington captain that July when still only nineteen. A further 3 Great Britain caps, against Australia, followed that autumn. Warrington's finances, however, were in a mess and so Sculthorpe was sold to St Helens that December in a world record deal for a forward, with Warrington receiving £300,000 plus the £70,000-rated Chris Morley.

At Knowsley Road, Sculthorpe has continued to improve and has been a key figure in the teams who have won the Super League Grand Final in 1999 and 2000, the Challenge Cup final in 2001 and the World Club Challenge in 2001. He was the 2001 Man of Steel and Great Britain's best player in the Guinness Ashes series. More honours for club and country seem inevitable. If only he were still at Warrington.

Charlie Seeling
Loose-forward, 1927-34

Season	Apps	Tries	Pts
1926/27	2	0	0
1927/28	16	4	12
1928/29	39	12	36
1929/30	29	2	6
1930/31	21	3	9
1931/32	30	3	9
1932/33	31	8	24
1933/34	27	9	27
TOTAL	**195**	**41**	**123**

Charlie Seeling was an important member of the Warrington side who twice won the Lancashire Cup (1929 and 1932) and twice suffered narrow defeats in Challenge Cup finals (1928 and 1933). He remains the greatest try-scoring loose-forward in the club's history, with 37 of his 41 touchdowns coming while he was wearing the number 13 jersey.

Seeling was the son of the famous All Black rugby union forward Charlie 'Bronco' Seeling, who later played for Wigan from 1909 to 1920. Seeling junior was two years old when his father brought him to England and he learned how to play rugby league with the Ince All Blacks, a Wigan junior side.

He joined Warrington in the 1926/27 season and made his Wire debut against Pontypridd at Wilderspool in April 1927. The following season, Warrington reached the Challenge Cup final against Swinton. It was the last final in the north before the move to Wembley and attracted a crowd of 33,909 to Wigan's Central Park.

Warrington, as usual, were the underdogs and were really battling against the odds when, in the days before substitutes, scrum-half Billy Kirk was carried off injured with Swinton leading 3-0. Seeling was moved out to the wing and scored a try in the corner to level matters at 3-3. Fate was against the gallant twelve men of Warrington, however, when, late in the game from a controversial scrum, a drop goal gave the trophy to Swinton 5-3.

Seeling tasted success when Warrington won the Lancashire Cup in November 1929 by beating Salford 15-2 and when they lifted the same trophy by beating St Helens 10-9 three years later. Both finals were staged at Central Park. Seeling also played in every round of the Challenge Cup as Warrington reached their first Wembley final in 1933, only to lose 21-17 to Huddersfield in a thrilling match.

After seven successful years at Warrington, he was transferred to Wigan for £200 and made 86 appearances for the Central Park club between 1934 and 1943. During the war he also played for Batley, Leeds and, most notably, Dewsbury, where he was a key forward in Eddie Waring's talented team.

Seeling died, aged eighty-eight, in March 1996.

Bill Shankland
Centre, 1931-38

Season	Apps	Tries	Goals	Pts
1931/32	36	23	4	77
1932/33	40	16	17	82
1933/34	34	14	0	42
1934/35	39	3	16	41
1935/36	32	6	22	62
1936/37	37	11	7	47
1937/38	13	1	4	11
TOTAL	231	74	70	362

One look at Bill Shankland's career statistics with Warrington will show what an exceptional rugby league player he was; he was an even better golfer. Shankland finished joint third in the Open Championship at St Andrews in 1939 and fourth at Royal Liverpool eight years later.

Shankland was born in Sydney in July 1907 and, as a young man, he swam and boxed for Australia and excelled on the track. He was also a fine cricketer and an outstanding rugby union fly-half, touring New Zealand, South Africa and, in 1926, the British Isles. Shankland then switched codes, and positions, and toured Great Britain as a centre with the 1929 Kangaroos, scoring 24 tries in 23 matches.

English rugby league clubs were queuing up to sign him and, at a time when miners were earning £2 10s per week, Warrington had to pay a £1,000 signing-on fee to secure his services.

When he arrived at Bank Quay Station in July 1931, more than 2,000 supporters were there to greet him and he quickly lived up to their expectations.

Shankland scored 23 tries in his first season and was appointed captain for the 1932/33 campaign. He quickly led Warrington to victory over St Helens in the Lancashire Cup final and became the first overseas skipper at Wembley, against Huddersfield in May 1933. Warrington lost 21-17 and suffered three more heartbreaking defeats on showpiece occasions, in the Championship finals of 1935 and 1937 and the Challenge Cup final of 1936.

Shankland did, however, collect a second Lancashire Cup winners' medal in October 1937 when Barrow were beaten 8-4 at Central Park with the mighty Australian kicking a goal. By then, Shankland was also the assistant professional at Haydock Park Golf Club and a second sporting career was beginning to take off. Shankland played his last Open in 1955, before turning a brash teenager named Tony Jacklin into a future champion and raising more than £200,000 for various charities.

Shankland's death was in keeping with his life. On the morning of Sunday 6 September 1998, aged ninety-one, he was feted at the Haydock Park Golf Club. That afternoon, he was the star of a parade of past players at the Wilderspool centenary match against Huddersfield. The following day he slipped and banged his head. He never regained consciousness.

Kelly Shelford
Loose-forward or stand-off, 1991-97

Season	Apps	Tries	Pts
1991/92	24(1)	4	16
1992/93	28	3	12
1993/94	34	13	52
1994/95	36(1)	12	48
1995/96	15	4	16
1996	10(3)	3	12
1997	28	5	20
TOTAL	175(5)	44	176

Shelford also kicked a goal and 8 drop goals.

Kelly Shelford was the creative kingpin in the Warrington side that just missed out on the title on points difference in 1994 and reached the Regal Trophy final in 1995. As well as scoring a good number of tries himself – especially during the 1993/94 and 1994/95 seasons – Shelford created many others with clever chip kicks. He was also at the heart of umpteen criss-cross moves involving centres like Allan Bateman and Jonathan Davies.

Shelford's best days were as a loose-forward (88 appearances), but he was also an effective stand-off (79 appearances). Shelford – who was a chunky 5ft 7in and 14st 12lb – signed for Warrington in June 1991 to replace Australian stand-off Chris O'Sullivan.

Shortly afterwards, he received a better offer from Bradford Northern and signed for them as well, but once that minor problem had been sorted out, Shelford became a wonderful servant for the club for seven seasons.

Before joining Warrington, Shelford, an Auckland player, had represented the Junior Kiwis and won 8 full New Zealand caps. He had also had a brief spell with Whitehaven in the 1989/90 season.

He was one of thirty players released by coach Darryl Van de Velde in the great player purge at the end of the 1997 season and he returned home to New Zealand. Former team-mate Mark Forster, now retired and coaching the Rylands Under-14 side, said: 'Kelly was very talented and a gifted footballer, ahead of his time really.

'I don't think he knew himself half the time what he was going to do. He had a superb pair of hands and he said to everybody "you run in the hole and I'll find you with the ball".

'He wasn't a good trainer, he did just enough, but he was at every session. I adopted his dog, Rolly, a British bulldog, when he went back to New Zealand.

'Kelly has got a courier business now, which is strange for him because he has to get up at 5 o'clock in the morning. Sometimes at Warrington he didn't get up until 5 o'clock in the afternoon!'

Frank Shugars
Forward, 1904-12

Season	Apps	Tries	Pts
1904/05	34	0	0
1905/06	25	0	0
1906/07	24	1	3
1907/08	26	2	6
1908/09	10	3	9
1909/10	35	7	21
1910/11	25	3	9
1911/12	33	2	6
TOTAL	**212**	**18**	**54**

Frank Shugars was a Welsh forward who became the first Warrington player to go on tour with Great Britain. Not only that, he went on the first Great Britain tour of Australia and New Zealand, an epic adventure which began when the party sailed from Tilbury on 15 April 1910 and did not end until the tourists arrived back at Plymouth on 16 September – five months later.

Shugars collected his only Great Britain cap during the trip, when he played for the 'Northern Union' against New Zealand in Auckland on 30 July. Northern Union won 52-20.

The tourists' record on the field (played 18, won 14, drew 1, lost 3, points for 527, points against 294) was more than commendable and would serve as a benchmark for all future tours. The tourists went home the way they had come, via Ceylon and Suez and the Mediterranean, aboard *RMS Otranto*. Their ship reached Plymouth on 16 September, and the next day they played a match at the ground of Plymouth Argyle, which was billed as England *v.* Wales and pulled in 5,000 curious Devonians.

Shugars was signed from the Penygraig rugby union club in 1904 in the days when rugby league, like union, was a fifteen-a-side game. He even played in Warrington's final fifteen-a-side match at home to Hunslet on the last day of the 1905/06 season before the administrators decided to do away with the flankers to make the game more open and exciting. It must have been a traumatic change for a forward, but Shugars adapted splendidly and played his best rugby in the new thirteen-a-side era.

Shugars was a wonderful servant to Warrington and played in two Challenge Cup-winning teams – in 1904/05 against Hull Kingston Rovers and again in 1906/07 against Oldham. While at Wilderspool, he also won 5 Welsh caps and made 2 appearances for Lancashire and one for Other Nationalities.

Arthur Skelhorne
Prop or loose-forward, 1911-25

Season	Apps	Tries	Pts
1910/11	9	2	6
1911/12	17	5	17*
1912/13	33	4	12
1913/14	23	2	6
1914/15	1	1	3
1918/19	6	2	6
1919/20	23	4	12
1920/21	27	10	30
1921/22	33	3	9
1922/23	35	8	24
1923/24	30	4	12
1924/25	22	4	12
TOTAL	**259**	**49**	**149**

*Skelhorne also kicked a goal.

Arthur Skelhorne was a Warrington prop-forward who was feared by the Australians. He played against the Kangaroos 7 times for Great Britain, England, Lancashire and Warrington and was only on the losing side once. With Skelhorne at number 10 and his Warrington team-mate Billy Cunliffe at number 8, Great Britain regained the Ashes in England in 1921 to start an incredible sequence of ten series victories which would stretch until 1950.

Skelhorne was also a member of the England, Lancashire and Warrington teams who beat the Australians during their 36-match tour of England and Wales in the 1921/22 season.

Skelhorne had joined Warrington from the Stockton Heath junior team in 1911. He received a £5 signing-on fee and so did his amateur club. It was money well spent.

His 7 Great Britain caps, 3 England caps and 6 appearances for Lancashire were mainly as a prop-forward, but for Warrington he was much more versatile. He played in every position from number 8 to number 13 and was even the club's leading try-scorer in the 1920/21 season, when he operated exclusively as a loose-forward.

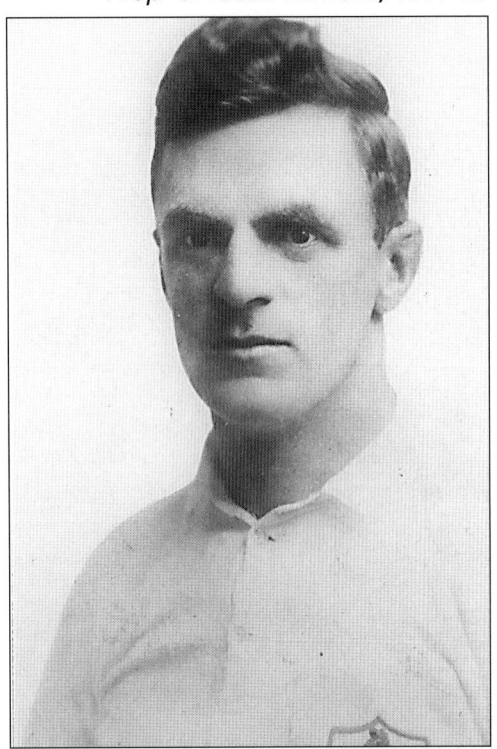

Skelhorne's international successes, however, were not mirrored in his domestic career. He only collected one medal, for the Challenge Cup final defeat against Huddersfield at Headingley in April 1913. Warrington lost 9-5 in front of 22,754 fans.

The Warrington team was: Ben Jolley; Ernie Brookes, Jim Tranter, Bert Renwick (captain), Bert Bradshaw; Syd Nicholas, Jim 'Shint' Daintith; George Thomas, J.W. Chesters, Arthur Skelhorne, Jim 'Scuddy' Fearnley, Richard Thomas and Harry Cox. Bradshaw scored a try and Jolley kicked a goal.

Skelhorne's standing within the game and inside the club was recognised for the 1924/25 season, when he was named as captain.

Kevin Tamati
Hooker, 1985-89

Season	Apps	Tries	Pts
1985/86	36(2)	2	8
1986/87	28(4)	1	4
1987/88	30(3)	2	8
1988/89	11(2)	1	4
TOTAL	**105(11)**	**6**	**24**

After his first few Test appearances for New Zealand against the Kangaroos, the Australian press nicknamed Kevin Tamati 'Terrible Tamati'. The journalists were not being disrespectful. They were using the word terrible as in Ivan the Terrible, the Russian Tsar – absolutely terrifying.

Rugby league writer and broadcaster Ray French summed it up best: 'Fiercely patriotic, Tamati hunted his opponents as if New Zealand's destiny itself depended upon every tackle made. He led charges in the middle of the field and, when through the opposition defence, he could lay off the ball to the backs with the skill and precision of a classy half-back.'

Tamati had mellowed, but only slightly, by the time he joined Warrington in August 1985, one month short of his thirty-second birthday. He was still a formidable competitor, however, and won his 22nd and final Kiwi cap against Great Britain in the drawn third Test at Elland Road that November.

At 5ft 10in and 15 stones, Tamati was ideally built for service in the front row, but it was not until Tony Barrow took over as Warrington's caretaker coach in March 1986 that he was switched to the number 9 jersey. It was an inspired move and the front row of Les Boyd, Kevin Tamati and Bob Jackson is still revered at Wilderspool.

All three scored tries as Warrington overwhelmed Halifax 38-10 to lift the Premiership Trophy in May 1986. Tamati scored a crucial try when the sides were locked at 10-10 just after half-time. After being hauled down close to the try line, Tamati played the ball to himself and crashed over to the delight of his team-mates and the travelling Wire fans.

Inevitably, Tamati pushed Boyd all the way for the Harry Sunderland man of the match award. Similarly, while he was with Widnes, Tamati had just been pipped by team-mate Joe Lydon for the Lance Todd prize as the Chemics defeated Wigan 19-6 in the 1984 Challenge Cup final.

When his playing days were over, Tamati worked as Warrington rugby league development officer and was in charge of the club's A team before being snapped up as Salford coach in October 1989. Tamati spent four years at the Willows, winning the Second Division title and Premiership, and he has also coached Chorley and Whitehaven.

George Thomas
Forward, 1903-14

Season	Apps	Tries	Goals	Pts
1903/04	33	2	0	6
1904/05	40	3	0	9
1905/06	38	5	1	17
1906/07	39	16	11	70
1907/08	31	2	44	94
1908/09	25	8	37	98
1909/10	34	3	30	69
1910/11	31	2	39	84
1911/12	39	1	19	41
1912/13	36	5	15	45
1913/14	36	0	3	6
1914/15	3	0	0	0
TOTAL	**385**	**47**	**199**	**539**

When George Thomas first arrived at Wilderspool in August 1903 from Newport Rugby Union Club, some members of the Warrington committee questioned his small stature for a forward: he was only 5ft 8in tall and weighed just 12st 11lb. Thomas replied by stating that: 'Good stuff lies in little room'. So it proved, as he made 385 appearances for Warrington, scoring 47 tries and kicking 199 goals for a tidy haul of 539 points.

He quickly became the crowd's favourite forward and a terror to opponents. A hard worker in the scrum and a fearless tackler, Thomas could always be found in the thick of the action.

He played in four Challenge Cup finals, collecting winners' medals in 1905 and 1907 and finishing on the losing side in 1904 and 1913. Thomas also set a club record which was to stand for ninety-one years when he scored 33 points in a match, from five tries and nine goals, as Warrington thrashed St Helens 78-6 in April 1909. The record stood until February 2000, when Lee Briers helped himself to 40 points in a Challenge Cup tie against York.

Thomas was outspoken, and that almost certainly cost him a place on the first Great Britain tour to Australia and New Zealand in 1910. When Warrington's first-team players went on strike in January 1914 over the non-payment of a £1 bonus, it was Thomas who addressed the 4,000-strong Wilderspool crowd after an A Team game to explain their grievances.

Thomas did, however, play in the first international rugby league match when he represented Wales against the touring New Zealand All Golds at Aberdare on 1 January 1908. Wales won 9-8 before a crowd estimated to be around 17,000 strong.

Following the outbreak of the First World War in August 1914, Thomas was one of the first to enlist and joined the South Lancashire Regiment. He continued to keep himself fit and won the five-mile race for his company. In April 1916, Thomas, who was a private, sent a letter to Harry Ashton, the former Warrington captain and secretary, at the Orford Hotel from the Western Front in France. Showing extreme candour and courage, he wrote: 'I have had some trying times on the football field and our side usually came out on top but as true as there is a

Cup kings: Warrington's Challenge Cup-winning team of 1907 at Wilderspool. From left to right, back row: I. Hackett (trainer), Frank Shugars, Alf Boardman, James Belton, George Heath, Bill Harmer, Frank Heesom (trainer). Middle row: Arthur Naylor, Ernie Brooks, Ike Taylor, Danny Isherwood, Jack Fish, Jimmy Tilley, Ernie Jordan, George Thomas. Front row: Tom Hockenhall, Sammy Lees.

drop of British blood runs through my veins I hope to give the Germans a sound thrashing.

'But if I should fall you can tell the boys I fell fighting like a hero should do for his King and country. We have had a rough time of it and have been constantly harassed by the Germans. Many comrades fell and twice I had narrow escapes. I helped on one occasion to carry my sergeant to a place of safety and bandage him up.'

In late June 1916, Thomas was made a colonel's orderly before, in the early hours of Monday 3 July 1916 he was killed in action on the Somme. An eyewitness reported that he was 'blown to pieces' by a German shell. He was just thirty-five and left a wife and young family, who lived at 12 Walton Road, Stockton Heath.

He was not forgotten at Wilderspool, however, and in March 1922 a benefit match raised £127 8s 11d for his widow. Thomas is also remembered on the internet, where he is listed under his full name, William George Thomas, on the web site organised by the Commonwealth War Graves Commission.

Memories of George Thomas were again revived in June 2000 when Warrington played London Broncos at Newport's Rodney Parade ground in an 'On the Road' Super League game. Warrington were led out by captain Allan Langer and mascot-for-the-day Ethan Thomas, aged ten, George's great-nephew. Ethan had won the honour in a *South Wales Argus* competition by nominating George as his favourite player.

122

Tommy Thompson
Winger, 1927-34

Season	Apps	Tries	Pts
1927/28	5	1	3
1928/29	27	17	51
1929/30	34	22	66
1930/31	42	28	84
1931/32	24	3	9
1932/33	37	26	78
1933/34	33	15	4
TOTAL	202	112	336

Thompson also kicked 14 goals.

Tommy 'Tubby' Thompson was a young winger from the Wigan area who beat the Kangaroos almost single-handedly. Thompson scored all the points, from three tries and four goals, as Warrington defeated Australia 17-8 at Wilderspool in December 1929 in front of 12,826 disbelieving spectators. He was also the first Warrington player to score six tries in a match and is one of only fifteen players who have scored more than 100 tries for the club.

As his nickname suggests, 'Tubby' was not built for speed. However, he possessed a wonderful sidestep, so that if he was close to the line with just one man to beat, a try could be guaranteed. Throughout his Warrington career, his regular centre was Great Britain international Billy Dingsdale and the pair became a formidable combination as they proved that Saturday afternoon against Australia.

However, it was Tommy Blinkhorn who was Thompson's centre when he scored six tries against Bradford Northern at Wilderspool in April 1933 as Warrington recorded a 38-12 victory.

While at Wilderspool, Thompson won an England cap and was a member of the Warrington team who won the Lancashire Cup in 1929 and again in 1932. He also collected a Challenge Cup losers' medal against Huddersfield at Wembley in May 1933. Thompson and Welsh winger Steve Ray were transferred to Oldham for £400 in September 1934. Thompson later spent two seasons at Leigh, from 1936-38, scoring 12 tries and 18 goals in 46 appearances.

But he will always be remembered as the man who beat Australia on his own. The full Warrington team that day was: Arthur Frowen; Tommy Blinkhorn, Les Perkins, Billy Dingsdale, Tommy Thompson; J.B. Griffiths, Billy Kirk; Billy Cunliffe, John Fisher, Jack Miller, Frank Mason, Frank Williams and Bill Jones.

Jim Tranter
Centre or back-row forward, 1911-28

Season	Apps	Tries	Pts
1911/12	24	3	9
1912/13	38	6	18
1913/14	25	2	6
1914/15	35	11	33
1918/19	15	9	27
1919/20	25	7	21
1920/21	37	7	21
1921/22	29	15	45
1922/23	34	12	36
1923/24	41	16	48
1924/25	34	7	21
1925/26	38	9	27
1926/27	34	10	30
1927/28	20	5	15
1928/29	10	1	3
TOTAL	**439**	**120**	**360**

Tranter also kicked 6 drop goals.

Jim Tranter scored 120 tries for Warrington, but he is best remembered as a devastating tackler. Tranter, who was 6ft 1in tall and weighed 14st, had long arms and perfected a type of tackle that became known far and wide as 'Tranter's Hook'. These days such a move would be classed as a high tackle and banned, because he became adept at allowing an opponent to almost go past him before whipping an arm across his neck to bring his progress to a shuddering halt.

Many an unsuspecting player thought he had beaten Tranter only to end up catapulted backwards. In fairness, though, Tranter only used his 'Hook' against opponents who had been dishing out punishment themselves without being penalised. Off the field, Tranter was a gentleman, being a strict teetotaller and a model professional.

Tranter, from Longford, signed for Warrington from the Newton amateur club as an eighteen-year-old in 1911. He received £5 and so did his club. He made his debut at the long defunct Ebbw Vale club that December, with his final appearance coming seventeen years later at Rochdale Hornets on Boxing Day 1928. While at Wilderspool, Tranter appeared in two Challenge Cup finals – as a centre against Huddersfield in 1913 and as a second-row forward against Swinton in 1928. On both occasions, however, Warrington suffered narrow defeats.

Tranter also played in the side who reached the Championship final for the first time, in May 1926, only to lose 22-10 to Wigan at Knowsley Road. He did taste success in the Lancashire Cup, however, when he played in the Warrington team who won the trophy for the first time by beating Oldham 7-5 at the Cliff.

Tranter was Warrington's leading try-scorer six times and captained the side in the 1923/24 season. His loyalty was recognised the following year, when he was awarded a testimonial match against Huddersfield, along with teammate Arthur Skelhorne, when he proved his versatility by playing at full-back.

His talents were also recognised by the selectors and he won 2 England caps and made 8 appearances for Lancashire.

Derek Whitehead
Full-back, 1969-79

Season	Apps	Goals	Pts
1969/70	26	83	166
1970/71	33(1)	85	170
1971/72	33	101	202
1972/73	36	135	270
1973/74	46	155	310
1974/75	31(2)	75	150
1975/76	22	47	94
1976/77	12(11)	21	42
1977/78	6(14)	11	22
1978/79	0(1)	0	0
TOTAL	**245(29)**	**713**	**1426**

Whitehead also kicked 21 drop goals and scored 17 tries, taking his points tally to an impressive 1516.

Only two Warrington players have won the Lance Todd Trophy as man of the match in the Challenge Cup final. Gerry Helme was the first, in 1950 and again in 1954, and Derek Whitehead was the second. Whitehead's finest hour came in the 1974 Challenge Cup victory over Featherstone Rovers at Wembley, when he kicked seven goals from all angles and distances in a 24-9 win. One week later, the Warrington full-back kicked two more goals in the 13-12 victory over St Helens in the Club Championship final at Central Park to equal Harry Bath's club record of 162 and round off an amazing season.

Whitehead played in 46 of Warrington's 51 games – more than any other player – and was also the man of the match when the Wire lifted their first trophy of the campaign, the Captain Morgan Trophy. Whitehead kicked two penalty goals – both from 45 yards – to seal a 4-0 victory over Featherstone on a cold, wet January afternoon at Salford. Six more goals came in the Player's No.6 Trophy success against Rochdale Hornets at Central Park two weeks later.

Whitehead's shared goalkicking record only survived until 1979, when Steve Hesford extended it to 170. On balance, Hesford was probably the better goalkicker, but Whitehead was much the better rugby player and was famous for his attacking runs and classic sidestep.

To prove the point, he won 3 Great Britain caps in 1971 – two against France and one against New Zealand – and made 5 appearances for Lancashire between 1973 and 1974. Whitehead, a butcher by trade, joined Warrington from Oldham in September 1969 when the club were struggling to recapture former glories. They were difficult days and the club almost went bust, but at least Whitehead was spared the nadir, the 50-0 home defeat by Salford in November 1970, being absent through injury.

The arrival of Alex Murphy in May 1971 transformed the club's fortunes and it seemed that Warrington were heading for Wembley in his first season in charge after victories over Batley, Castleford and Bramley earned a Challenge Cup semi-final place against St Helens.

Running man: Derek Whitehead follows up his own kick to score a try against Rochdale Hornets in the 1974 Player's No. 6 Trophy final at Central Park.

Three weeks before the big game, however, Whitehead was injured in a car crash, suffering nasty cuts about the face and hands, and could not play. Even without Whitehead, Warrington took the Saints to a replay, but lost the second game 10-6 on a Wednesday night in front of a crowd of 32,180.

Whitehead, who stood at 5ft 10in and 13st, was back to his best the following season, kicking 135 goals and a drop goal, as Warrington claimed the League Leaders' rose bowl, their first trophy for five years. The 1973/74 campaign, of course, would be even better for Whitehead and the Wire. Both returned to Wembley against Widnes in 1975, only to suffer a heartbreaking 14-7 defeat with Whitehead kicking two goals.

He continued to serve the club as a player and, later, as a member of the coaching staff and in 1979/80 he was awarded a benefit season. Warrington coach Billy Benyon wrote in his testimonial brochure: 'Derek was a truly thinking footballer, capable of turning a match. His ability has always been unquestioned in the professional rugby game, a truly great competitor, and one of the finest goal-kicking full-backs that rugby league has known.'

Frank Williams
Second-row forward, 1921-34

Season	Apps	Tries	Pts
1921/22	1	0	0
1922/23	19	2	6
1923/24	33	6	18
1924/25	28	3	9
1925/26	39	17	51
1926/27	38	10	30
1927/28	37	15	45
1928/29	39	15	45
1929/30	42	6	18
1930/31	34	3	9
1931/32	10	2	6
1932/33	13	4	12
1933/34	19	4	12
TOTAL	**352**	**87**	**261**

Until Harry Bath and Bob Eccles came along, Frank Williams was the greatest try-scoring forward in the club's history. What's more, his total of 87 tries in 352 appearances still marks him out as a quality player almost seventy years after he retired.

Williams was a local lad who was discovered in 1921 while playing in the Warrington Works Competition, a tournament that unearthed a lot of talent in years gone by. Williams was spotted playing for Cheshire Lines and was quickly signed up for £25, a more than respectable sum at the time. He made his Wire debut at Hunslet in November 1921, but it was not until the following season that he established himself in the side. Most of his career was spent in the second row, but he also made a number of appearances as a loose-forward and, later, at prop.

Williams was in his prime in the four seasons from 1925 to 1929, when he scored 57 tries in 153 games and played in two major finals. Sadly, the 1926 Championship final against Wigan and the 1928 Challenge Cup final against Swinton both ended in narrow defeats.

Another disappointment arrived when Williams missed out on the Great Britain tour to Australia and New Zealand in 1928, despite producing a superb performance in the trial game. Williams won his solitary England cap against Other Nationalities at St Helens in October 1930 to add to the Lancashire cap he had collected against Cumberland three years earlier.

The only winners' medal of his career came in the Lancashire Cup in November 1929, when Salford were beaten 15-2 in the final at Wigan's Central Park in front of a 21,000 crowd. He wore his medal with pride for many years after he had retired.

Williams and fellow forward Frank Mason were awarded a joint testimonial match in the 1932/33 season, which raised £89/12/6 pence for each player. His record haul of tries for a Warrington forward stood for twenty-two years until it was finally beaten by Harry Bath in 1956.

John Woods
Stand-off, 1987-89

Season	Apps	Tries	Goals	Pts
1987/88	37	13	147	351*
1988/89	35	12	107	262
TOTAL	72	25	254	613

Wood also kicked 5 drop goals.

When he signed for Warrington from Bradford Northern for £40,000 in June 1987, John Woods had already won 10 caps for Great Britain, but Wire fans were still unprepared for just what a graceful and talented player he was. Club chairman Peter Higham admitted as much when he presented Woods with the player of the year award at the annual dinner at the end of the 1987/88 season. 'I wish we had signed him years ago,' said Higham – if only Warrington had.

Woods had made his name with his hometown club, Leigh, scoring 2,172 points from 135 tries, 859 goals and 11 drop goals from 1976 to 1985, before spending two seasons with Bradford.

Travelling back and forth across the Pennines, however, was starting to become a burden and so Woods jumped at the chance of joining coach Tony Barrow at Wilderspool. Woods, who was almost thirty-one at the time, was rejuvenated by the move, so much so that he quickly won his 11th Great Britain cap as a substitute against Papua New Guinea at Wigan in October 1987. The way he accumulated points in that 1987/88 season almost defied belief and he finished the campaign with 351 – just 12 short of Harry Bath's club record.

Warrington made a poor start to the following season, but Woods helped to raise spirits by inspiring the team to victory in the British Coal Nines at Central Park. Warrington beat Wigan 12-6, St Helens 6-0 and the Rest of the World 24-0 in the final to lift the trophy, with Woods deservedly named man of the tournament.

By now, Woods' one remaining ambition was to play at Wembley and he came agonisingly close in the spring of 1989 as Warrington beat Halifax, Keighley and Hull KR to set up a semi-final meeting with Wigan at Maine Road.

Injuries forced new coach Brian Johnson to play Woods in the unaccustomed position of scrum-half and he responded by kicking three excellent penalty goals to give Warrington a 6-4 lead after 60 minutes. Joe Lydon then broke Warrington hearts with a penalty and a record-breaking drop goal from 61 yards to pave the way for a 13-6 victory for Wigan.

Woods was the players' player of the year for the 1988/89 season and it was a major surprise when he was sold to nouveau riche Rochdale Hornets for £50,000 in July 1989. Players with the sublime skills of John Woods do not come along too often.